Published in cooperation
with the National Park Service and the
U.S. Department of Interior.

Alaska Natural History Association
750 West Second Avenue, Suite 100
Anchorage, Alaska 99501

Alaska Natural History Association is a non-profit organization dedicated to enhancing the understanding and conservation of Alaska's natural, cultural, and historical resources of Alaska's public lands.

ISBN 0-9602876-1-2

Second Printing 1980
Third Printing 1992
Fourth Printing 1997
Fifth Printing 2000

Printed by Pyramid Printing, Anchorage, Alaska
on recycled, chlorine-free stock using soy inks

CARVED HISTORY

This booklet was compiled for Sitka National Historical Park and Alaska Natural History Association by Marilyn R. Knapp with the assistance of Mary P. Meyer. It was edited by Susan F. Edelstein. Vesta Dominicks is to be thanked for her assistance with the spelling of many of the Tlingit words in the manuscript. Many valuable sources were used, principally from the park files and library. One source, however, deserves special acknowledgment: Andrew Hope III's manuscript, Sacred Forms, provided excellent information on the park's poles and was unique in its interpretation from the Tlingit point of view.

Pen and ink illustrations by **JoAnn George.**

Introduction

"In the old days..." is the way many of today's Tlingit elders begin their stories. In the old days, the way of life was based on the rich natural resources of southeast Alaska, on respect for all living things, and on a unique and complex social structure.

Totem poles are a reflection of these ways. They are bold statements making public record of the lives and history of the people who had them carved, and represent pride in clans and ancestors. They mark the success and renown of families.

"In the old days" the poles were not found along a neat lane, as they are now in Sitka. Step back in time and see them as they used to stand. Imagine yourself a trader on a European ship plying these waters during the early 19th century fur trade era. Ahead, close by the water, on the shore of a sheltered bay, is a row of single story rectangular cedar houses. The green mantle of the rain forest is close behind them, and the misty mountains rise above. Canoes are pulled up along the beach and people are busy preparing to come out to the ship to trade.

Towering above them, at the corners and in front of the houses, are carved poles whose striking design and colors proclaim the identities and stories of the villagers —if only you could read them. "If only..." is a problem for us today. In many instances, we do not know enough about the people or the poles to satisfy our interest.

We do know that poles stood along the village fronts of the Haida and Tlingit Indians of northern British Columbia and extreme southeast Alaska, and that carved house posts were used by the Tlingit farther north. The name "totem" is not a local word, but is an Algonquin Indian term describing crests showing natural objects or animals that represent a family group. "Totem" can refer to an individual crest, as well as a whole pole.

To begin to understand totem poles, it is necessary to know that the Tlingit and Haida people are each divided into two major groups called moieties represented by the raven and the eagle in totem art. Within these major divisions are numerous clans. Each clan shares legends, crests or symbols, ancestors, and artifacts, and clan membership is an important source of identification and pride. This system exists today, although many Native traditions are less closely followed than in the past.

Totem poles generally serve one of four purposes: crest poles give the ancestry of a particular family; history poles record the history of a clan; legend poles illustrate folklore or real life experiences; and memorial poles commemorate a particular individual. Their first recorded sightings were by European explorers and traders in the late 18th century, although the art form existed prior to contact.

A totem is traditionally carved by an artist of a clan opposite the clan of the person who commissions it. Special occasions among the Tlingit sometimes prompt large celebrations that have come to be called potlatches. New poles often were erected as part of the festivities, or were sometimes themselves the cause for a potlatch. Although missionaries and civil government had almost wiped out large potlatches before World War I, a contemporary version is evolving.

Craftsmen in Cedar: Totems as an Art Form

The carving of bone, wood, and stone is an ancient and distinctive art among the people of the Northwest Coast. Their love of beauty may first have been expressed by the carving of utilitarian objects such as ladles, bowls, and boxes, and later developed into the monumental totem poles. Carving continues to evolve today as artists, like those at the park's Cultural Center, teach the craft and produce the works of art.

It is believed the earliest "totem poles" were structural interior house posts; next to be developed may have been posts at the exterior corners of clan houses. Detached, exterior poles reached their zenith in the late 19th century.

Totem pole carving was traditionally the responsibility of a select group of craftsmen who had been formally trained in an apprenticeship system. The totem craftsman was commissioned by the opposite clan when a large totem, house post, or special memorial pole was needed. The desired size, symbols, and story were related to him in full detail, and he would then carve the pole.

Study of Northwest Coast Indian art shows that style is usually based on the formline which scholar Bill Holm describes as a curving, swelling, and diminishing line that establishes the principal shapes and design units within a piece of art. It is this formline that makes two-dimensional art forms seem to take on a third dimension. The formline is painted before carving begins.

The general layout of a totem pole is essentially a two-dimensional formline wrapped around a half cylinder. This is especially true of Haida totem poles. With the use of formline, abstract representations of creatures, either natural or supernatural, can be constructed on flat surfaces.

If painted, the formline is either black or red. Its proportions run from thick to thin and usually travel in a curvilinear pattern to connect and outline the three principal elements found in the art: the ovoid, "U", and "S" shapes.

Black is used on areas to be accented, such as eye pupils, eyelid lines, eyebrows, and claws, as well as in primary formlines. Red is used on lips, nostrils, sometimes bodies, and as a secondary formline element in two-dimensional areas. Blue is used in eye sockets and in two-dimensional design areas.

Early Tlingit and Haida poles are often distinguishable by their layout. Haida figures interconnect and overlap more than Tlingit figures, which are often isolated from each other and present a more rounded and sculptured appearance.

Originally, all paints were made from natural materials, usually consisting of pulverized minerals with masticated salmon eggs and saliva used as a binder. Red was usually obtained from hematite, black from graphite, and the blue/green blends from copper. Soot was used to change the hue of other colors.

In the late 18th century totem carvers began to trade for dry pigments which were then mixed with the natural ones. Today most carvers use commercial paints, although some experiment with the traditional mixtures.

Many older poles throughout Alaska have been repainted using modern paints and non-traditional colors. Several poles in this park were repainted in this manner, although the paint has been removed in most cases.

How the Totem Poles Came to Sitka

In June 1890, President Benjamin Harrison set aside, as a public park, the historic site of the Kiks.ádi Tlingit fort at the mouth of Indian River in Sitka, the forerunner of today's national historical park. John G. Brady, Alaska's fifth territorial governor, had a great interest in Native people and their cultures, and may have influenced President Harrison's decision. Largely through Governor Brady's efforts, eighteen of the poles in this park were collected and placed here. Most are Haida in origin and none are originally from Sitka.

The first poles received for the park are described by the following synopsis of 1902 news articles from Sitka's *THE ALASKAN.*

The tall totem pole that was presented to the people of Alaska by Chief Son-i-hat of Kasaan now stands in Indian River Park along with four house posts that were also the gift of Son-i-hat. The big pole was erected during the past week by the crew of the Revenue Cutter *Richard Rush,* assisted by George Kostrometinoff and a gang of prisoners from the jail. Son-i-hat, a Haida chief, presented the pole, the house posts, a war canoe, and a big log community house to the people of the District of Alaska through Governor John G. Brady. The big totem is more than seventy years old and time and the elements left their marks, but trimming away about a half-inch of the surface has removed most of these. The pole was painted by Klay-nay-hoo, known as Jim the Jeweler, before it was erected at the park.

The U.S. Revenue Cutter *Rush* also played an important role in gathering other poles placed here in the park. Congress, in 1903, appropriated $50,000 for Alaska's participation in the Louisiana Purchase Exposition on St. Louis. Brady gathered 20 totem poles from Prince of Wales Island, about 125 miles south of Sitka. Although the exact sources are not clear, both *Rushs* log and Governor Bradys report indicate that sources included the Tlingit villages Tuxekan and Klawock, and the Haida villages of Howkan, Klinkwan, Sukkwan, Old Kasaan, and Koinglas.

Some recarving, patching, and repainting was done and the poles were shipped to St. Louis. After the fair, some totems were in such poor condition that they were sold. The remaining poles were sent to the Lewis and Clark Exposition in Portland, and then shipped back to Sitka aboard the steamer *Alki* in 1905.

Sitka photographer and artist E.W. Merrill supervised the erection of the totems at carefully selected sites in the park. Contemporaries recall his repairing and painting the poles, often at his own expense.

In 1922 the National Park Service arranged for the Alaska Road Commission to supervise the park, which had been proclaimed Sitka National Monument by President William Howard Taft in 1910 and placed in the National Park System in 1916. Peter Trierschield, a Sitka resident, was appointed caretaker, and his period of service was a constant battle against rot and deterioration.

In April 1938, Alaska Territorial Governor John Troy wrote the Director of the National Park Service suggesting a rehabilitation program for the poles through the Civilian Conservation Corps (CCC) program. The project began in 1939 with Native artisans doing the repair and restoration work.

This and other repair projects, although extending the life of some of the poles, created problems from the perspective of today's historians and curators. It is believed that designs were altered slightly each time the poles were copied or repaired, so that today's poles may differ significantly from those produced by the original artists. A second problem has been the loss or decay of pieces of poles either completely or partially recarved in the CCC project. For a time the poles lay along the trail in the park, next to their reproductions. In an attempt to salvage them, they were placed at the Sitka Naval Air Station on Japonski Island in 1942. Unfortunately, poor storage conditions led to continued decay, and only a few poles and fragments survive today. The original poles and fragments are displayed in the Totem Exhibit Hall in the park visitor center.

The origin of many of the poles in Sitka National Historical Park remains a mystery due to incomplete and confusing records. The best method for tracing them is to learn the clan affiliations of residents of the villages at the time the poles were collected and then find corresponding crests or legends on the totems. The legends and history depicted by the poles come from the oral history of the Tlingit and Haida people; in some cases they remain the secret property of a family or clan. Because of the passage of time, civil and missionary pressures on Natives to abandon their traditional culture, and physical alterations to the poles, it is difficult, often impossible, to document or clearly understand legends associated with them.

Interpreting Totems

A stroll through the park, with particular attention paid to aesthetics, will provide a taste of the skills of these creative and talented artists, of their forest and ocean world, and of their respect for every living thing in it. The brief narratives in this booklet describe the individual poles as well as records allow. In some cases the records are conflicting; in others there is little or nothing available. That scant amount, however, has helped many visitors deepen their understanding of the Tlingit and Haida people of southeast Alaska.

Interpretation of totem poles must be approached with caution. Though the stylized features of Raven, Eagle, or Beaver can be easily recognized on a pole, a deeper, more thorough knowledge of the Native peoples and their history is necessary to properly interpret any pole's story. When an animal, usually Raven, is referred to by a proper noun, that animal plays the role of a legendary cultural hero with human characteristics in that particular context. Lower case references usually refer to the animal in a generic sense. Many of the stories and events associated with totem poles have been lost over time. Others are interpreted differently by different clans and communities.

The Future of the Park Totem Poles

Most of the totems now standing along the park's trails are reproductions of the original poles that Governor Brady collected and brought to Sitka. The Brady Poles were representative of the totemic art form and embodied the cultural heritage of the native people of this region. Although each reproduction is reflective of the style and interpretation of its carver, they have generally remained true to the original poles.

Over the years the park staff have utilized a variety of methods to preserve the standing poles and original pole fragments remaining in the park collection. As new preservation methods and technologies are developed, they will be evaluated and applied by the park to preserve the integrity of the collection. Questions remain concerning whether to continue to carve totem poles for the park and, if so, whether to carve reproduction poles as the old poles come down or create new poles by contemporary carvers. The Totems evoke images and traditions of a time past, yet the culture and art forms continue to evolve.

Visitor Center Exhibits

Among the physical expressions of Tlingit culture are house post totem poles, Chilkat blanket weaving, spruce root basketry, button blankets, metal shields, jewelry, and beadwork. Tlingits live in close association with the land and the animals of the forest and the sea, as evidenced by the art forms that are on exhibit in the lobby. Today the way of life of the Tlingit has changed so much that some elders worry about perpetuation of clan property. To preserve these artifacts and to keep them in Sitka, several custodians have chosen to place selected objects in the visitor center at Sitka National Historical Park.

Although this publication is limited to wooden totems, the park staff will be pleased to provide information about other objects on display.

The Liuknax.adi Frog Sculpture

This sculpture is a frog emblem carved for the Coho people by Kaagwaantaan artist John Silverman for the 1904 potlatch. It is a copy of one destroyed earlier by Kiks.ádi people who disputed the Coho people's use of the frog crest. The Coho people claim that the crest is based on an event during the construction of a new clan house in Klukwan many years ago when they discovered a giant frog underground.

Erected in the Coho frog house in Sitka, the sculpture was rigged to bow whenever anyone opened the front door. The Frog and the Sleeping Man pole to its right are part of the late Frank Kitka's collection; they were placed on display in the visitor center in 1971 by his heirs.

Sleeping Man Legend Pole

At the top of this pole are two salmon, symbols of the Coho Salmon clan, a subdivision among the Tlingit Indians of the Raven family. The faces below the coho salmon represent the village people killed by the octopus. Sleeping Man is the next figure. The octopus is the face at the base of the pole, with its tentacles extending up to Sleeping Man and the Coho people. The face in the center is Sleeping Man's slave. The animals above and below the slave represent bear, the emblem of the slave.

This pole is an example of a legend pole, one that tells a story. It differs in this way from a crest, history, or memorial pole.

The Coho people were drying sockeye salmon and the red color of the fish attracted a giant octopus. The octopus attacked the people and wiped out the village. One of the Coho people, a man called Sleeping Man, was away hunting with his slave at the time. When he returned to the village and saw the destruction, he was very distressed. He vowed he would try to attract the octopus again so that he could get revenge. After a great deal of unsuccessful effort, he finally succeeded in attracting the octopus with red blankets. As the octopus approached, Sleeping Man got into his canoe and paddled out to meet it. He tied a dagger to his hand and stepped out onto the octopus. In the struggle that followed, both Sleeping Man and the octopus were killed. Sleeping Man was a hero and in memory of him and his deed this totem pole was carved.

Kaagwaantaan Wolf House Posts

The large house post across from the windows is known as Painting Wolf. It is a replica of a very old house post and is the crest of the Kaagwaantaans.

Much of the history and identity of the clan is told through the totem figures. Abalone shell inlay is an outstanding feature of this house post. This use of shell indicated wealth; it was a trade item from the Indians of the Oregon and California coasts.

The large wolf in a sitting position holds a little wolf in his paws. The little wolf represents the importance of future generations of the clan. The tongue extended to him represents the transfer of knowledge.

Several explanations are given for the three inverted heads on the house post. One interpretation is that they represent three clans whose members came to the potlatch.

The two posts on the reception desk wall are known as Multiplying Wolf. Use of copper indicates clan wealth and prestige, since it was obtained by trading with the Copper River Indians to the north. The two young wolves facing each other at the bottom signify the time the clan outgrew its clan house and had to move to new houses.

These three house posts are spruce, rather than the more typical cedar. Prepared for the last big potlatch given by the Tlingits in southeast Alaska in 1904, they were carved for the respected leader *Anaxóots*. The posts were in his clan house until it was torn down in 1959.

These Kaagwaantaan house posts are displayed through the generosity of the Gooch Hit (Wolf House) in Sitka. Please refrain from commercial photography without special permission.

Kaagwaantaan Mother Eagle House Posts

These four similar posts are from inside the Eagle Nest House of the Kaagwaantaan clan in Sitka, and may be about 200 years old.

Their design depicts the Mother Eagle story, in which a young eagle brings fish from the sea to feed a girl and her grandmother who are the only survivors of a terrible sickness among the members of the clan. The girl had taught the eagle to believe she was its mother. The girl survives, matures, and marries a man from the opposite moiety, and Kaagwaantaan children are born, ensuring the survival of the clan.

All of these posts illustrate the Mother Eagle in slightly different forms, each sitting atop a round figure with a face that represents her nest. The face in the nest tells, in totem art, that it too has life and should be respected, for the Tlingit feel that there is life in everything.

The posts on the left are more decorative than those on the right and were displayed in the back of the house where the highcaste people and important visitors spent their time. Like all house posts, these stood inside and were structurally important in supporting the clan house roof. The notches cut in the tops show where the main roof poles rested.

These house posts are displayed through the generosity of the Kaagwaantaan clan of Sitka.

Outdoor Totems

To see the totem poles along the Governor's Walk, leave the lobby through the double doors facing Sitka Sound and follow the trail to your left. Before stepping out of the lobby be sure to look up at the Kaagwaantaan (Wolf) Clan house front above the doors.

The one-mile loop trail begins here and ends with the cluster of poles at the visitor center entrance. Match each pole with the line illustrations in the book.

Also along the trail is the site of the 1804 Kiks.ádi fort and battleground that marked the last major Native resistance to Russian domination. This historic site is the reason the park was originally set aside.

Yaadaas Crest Pole

This pole is from the house of *Dzeilu* in the Haida village of Kasaan. The two human figures on top are called Village Watchmen, and are used in many Haida and some Tlingit carvings. These watchmen kept vigil for enemies. The figure below is Raven with his tongue reaching down to a bear-like figure. One source indicates this is a symbol of transference of knowledge. The next figure, a bear, holds a human form which is, in turn, changing into an animal. The bottom figure is also a bear. The bear and Raven are both crests of the Yaadaas clan of Kasaan.

Yaadaas Crest Corner Pole

This pole stood at one of the exterior corners of the Yaadaas clan house. The human figure at the top is the Village Watchman. Below the Watchman is Raven in Human Form. The next figure is also Raven, while the base figure appears to be a bear holding an animal of some type in its mouth. Figures below the Village Watchman may be crests of the clan who owned the house, and could represent incidents in the real or mythical history of the clan.

This pole is a copy carved by Tlingit artist Tommy Jimmy in 1978 to replace the original collected in 1903. It is believed to be a crest pole portraying, as does the Yaadaas Crest Pole, the heraldic emblems of the Yaadaas clan of Old Kasaan. Fragments of the original pole remain in the possession of the National Park Service.

In the past, this pole was referred to as First Twin, since it and the Pole on Page 19, portray the same figures and are from the same house.

Wolf Pole

This pole is named for the prominent wolf totem at its center. It appears to be Tlingit in the style of carving, but its origin and meaning are unclear. The original pole was collected from Prince of Wales Island in 1903 and withstood many years of patching and repairing. A reproduction pole was carved in 1982 by Reggie Peterson.

This is probably a crest pole. The top figure is a man, perhaps the Village Watchman or the pole's owner. Next is a wolf, recognized by its pointed ears. The bottom figure is a salmon. The wolf and salmon may represent clan crest symbols or they may represent the clan crests of a husband and wife. One interpretation of the pole identifies the salmon as sockeye and suggests it symbolizes a legend of a boy who was captured by the Dog Salmon people.

Memorial/ Mortuary Column

Memorial and mortuary columns were common pole types found in southeast Alaska. In early days, the dead were sometimes cremated. The back side of a mortuary column often had a hole used as a receptacle for the ashes of the honored dead. A mortuary or memorial column was usually topped by a single figure indicating the clan or moiety of the person interred or honored.

There seems to be a fine distinction between memorial and mortuary poles. The mortuary pole was an actual column of interment, while the memorial pole was a column of rememberance. In some instances a memorial pole was raised to honor a living person.

The similarities in construction and appearance of these two types of poles make it difficult to determine their original purpose.

Though the totem at the top of this column is similar to Raven in form, the feathers on the back of the head and wings and the length of the beak suggest a cormorant. This pole is a 1979 copy of one collected by Brady in 1903; the original is being preserved by the National Park Service.

Frog/Raven Pole

Although some interpretations describe this as a legend pole, showing Raven as the mischief maker, other sources indicate that it is a Haida crest pole, possibly from Sukkwan, displaying the raven and the frog crests of the people there. Unfortunately, little information on its origin is available.

Through the years, many techniques have been used to preserve the totem poles. Since they were originally placed in the park in 1906, many have been patched with insert work, rotted surfaces have been trimmed away, features have been reshaped to eliminate decayed areas, and fresh coats of paint have been applied.

The original Frog/Raven column was patched, trimmed, and painted, but by 1939, park records state: "It is doubtful if it can be repaired, for when it dries out for working, it may fall apart." This replica was carved during the early 1940's, reportedly by George Benson and John Sam.

Yaadaas Crest Corner Pole

Nathan Jackson carved this reproduction pole in 1982. Compare this pole with its "twin" on page 15.

Totem pole carving, as described by Edward Keithahn in *Monuments in Cedar,* was prescribed art: "The carver as an artist had little if any personal liberty in his work, his contribution being skill and dexterity and a knowledge of the traditional style. He was told exactly what was to be carved on the monument, and traditional style...dictated the style and manner in which the conventionalized figures would appear in the sculpture." Therefore, it is possible that different artists could have carved two original poles producing pieces almost identical in appearance.

The figures on this pole are the Village Watchman, Raven in Human Form, Raven, and a bear.

Trader Legend Pole

This is an example of a ridicule pole, a type of legend pole usually erected to notify everyone of an unpaid debt. The top figure represents a white man, indicated by the use of curly hair and a beard. Perhaps he is a trader who cheated the Haida. The next figure is holding a shrimp in its mouth, a symbol said to represent a thief. The next figure is a crab, also a symbol of thievery. The bottom figure is a beaver, recognized by its teeth and tail. The pole originally stood in the Haida village of Sukkwan. It may have belonged to the clan of that village which claimed the beaver as its crest, or stealing beaver pelts may have been this man's transgression. A photograph of the pole at its Sukkwan site is found in *Monuments in Cedar* by Edward Keithahn.

Erosion and decay took their toll on the original, and this replica was carved in the 1938-42 CCC project.

An interesting sidelight is that while this copy was being made in Sitka, a local story involving an unfair trader grew around it. That story has become so real to some local residents that the pole is assumed to be a Sitka original.

Raven Memorial Pole

Raven is portrayed on this memorial column, distinguished by his rather large, slightly crooked beak. The carving is in the style and is believed to have come from the village of Tuxekan. This copy was carved by George Federoff, after the original was accidentally burned in 1959.

In Sitka, the Tlingits placed their memorial poles on the ridge behind their village (along present-day Katlian Street) overlooking the channel.

Memorial poles, along with house posts, are among the oldest forms of totem poles. The narrative on page 17 gives detailed information about them.

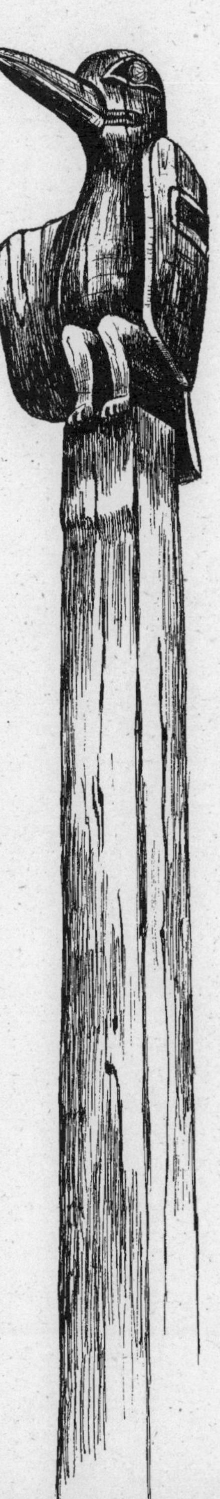

Gaanaxadi/ Raven Crest Pole

This is a 1983 reproduction of the original pole collected from the Tlingit village of Tuxekan. Tlingit artist Nathan Jackson and noted carver Steve Brown used early photographs by E.W. Merrill from the park collection to reproduce the details of the original pole.

It is unclear whether this is a story pole or a crest pole. One legend, called "Raven and the Whale," is suggested by the figure of the whale near the center of the pole.

In that story, Raven somehow found himself inside a whale. Hungry, he lit a fire, thinking he might eat some parts of the whale. The whale soon died, and eventually floated ashore with Raven trapped inside. When he heard the voices of the villagers approaching the beached whale, Raven began making noise. The villagers became curious about the noise, and cut open the whale. Raven quickly stepped out, hungry as always, and tricked the villagers into leaving him lots of food.

Lakich'inei Pole

The origin of this pole is unknown. Although the top figure is the subject of an ancient Tlingit legend, there is some evidence that the pole came from a Haida village. It has been suggested that Haida carvers learned of crests and legends of the Tlingit through intermarriage, and sometimes incorporated them into poles carved for their own villages.

Lakich'inei, the top figure, is pressing one of his children, who was half-human and half-dog, against his coat made from the spine of a fish, killing the child.

The mid-pole figure appears to be Bear Who Married a Woman, also a legend found among the Tlingit, and the bottom figure is Bear with a snail or shrimp-like creature in his mouth.

Park records from 1939 indicate large areas of decay in the original pole but do not state whether it was replaced or has survived until today.

Mosquito Legend Pole

A totem pole carver was a professional artist, and a fine craftsman's reputation could spread throughout the region. Among the people of northern British Columbia and southeast Alaska, Haida carvers were considered most accomplished and commissions could come from Tlingit as well as Haida villages. This pole could have been produced under such circumstances.

Although Haida in design and topped by the familiar Village Watchman, a Tlingit figure, *Gooteekhl*, associated with the creature from which mosquitoes originated, is the second totem on this pole. Below the mosquito is a bear, while the bottom figure is probably a devilfish or octopus, recognized by the suction cups used as eyebrows.

This pole, a copy of the original, was recarved by Frank Kitka in the 1938-41 CCC project.

The following is a synopsis of the mosquito legend as told in John Swanton's *Tlingit Myths and Texts:*

An unusual child was born to a chief's daughter, not exactly human in form, for he had sharp arrow points on his head. One day, the mother angered him, and he killed her by driving the arrow points into her breasts. Afterward he fled into the woods, where he continued to kill other villagers out hunting or collecting wood.

One of the village men, the boy's uncle, set a trap for the boy and succeeded in wounding him with a poison arrow. His uncle trapped him by following his blood stains and eventually found him. The boy protested and pleaded for his life, but his uncle killed him for having destroyed so many villagers. The boy's body was burned, leaving only ashes. These ashes were driven about by the wind and became the mosquitoes that still torment people today.

Saanaheit Pole and House Posts

Rising more than 50 feet, this pole is a copy of a pole given to Governor John Brady in 1901 by Saanaheit, a resident of the village of Old Kasaan. The original of this very tall pole may have been an entrance pole, because of the small hump at the base that could indicate the top of a door opening. A Sitka newspaper article from 1902 states that the pole was then more than 70 years old. It was repaired in Governor Brady's sawmill, shipped to the 1904 St. Louis Exposition, then to the 1905 Lewis and Clark Exposition in Portland, Oregon, and finally back to Sitka. During the CCC project, when it was about 110 years old, the pole was lowered, laid out alongside a new cedar log (made by joining two large logs), and a copy was carved using the designs of the original pole. Although several figures such as the traditional Village Watchman, a bear, and Raven are identifiable, other figures are not, and little information about this intricately carved giant has survived.

The four short poles are indoor house posts and are also gifts from *Saanaheit* to Governor Brady. The notches in the tops were cut to receive the large log beams of the house. These posts were placed at the corners of the large, single story dwelling. Illustrations on the house posts are said to be from a legend in which Raven obtains the sun, moon, and stars for the people of the earth. The original posts were brought to Sitka from Kasaan in 1901, and were reproduced by Reggie Peterson in 1981.

Raven/ Shark Pole

There are differing versions of the meaning and origin of this pole, though it appears to be Tlingit. Clans in Tuxekan, the Tlingit community from which the pole may have come, claim the totem figures carved here as their crests.

The figures on the pole appear to be, from top to bottom, Raven, a shark or dogfish, a wolf or fox, and a bear or stump. In some instances, a bear used as the base figure on the totem pole symbolizes that the story had its origin at the beginning of time.

In 1964 the original Raven/Shark Pole was part of the Alaska Exhibit at the New York World's Fair. By 1978 that pole had decayed and was replaced by a copy carved by Tommy Jimmie.

The following is one version of a Tlingit Raven/Shark legend:

In ancient times all animals understood each other and used common language. Raven was on a beach. He went underwater and traveled until he came upon a large village. This village was in another world. In the middle of the village was a large house with mostly women and children inside. The houses were very large. On the upper level of one of the houses was a very nice looking lady. As Raven looked at her she became more beautiful. He could not take his eyes off her. A little boy ran by the fire. Raven called him over, asked who the woman was and told him he wanted to talk to her. The little boy replied that she was his sister. He told the boy to tell the sister that he liked her. The boy relayed the message and returned to tell Raven that his sister thought he was attractive too, and that he was the kindest visitor to come to the house and he seemed to be a sensible man. Raven then said that he wanted to marry her. The lady cried and told the boy that though she would like to marry him she was ashamed of her body and that her face was her only beautiful feature. Raven replied that beauty is nothing, that man looks for inner beauty that radiates from the face. The boy relayed this to his sister and she married Raven soon thereafter.

Bicentennial Pole

A design competition in honor of the Nation's Bicentennial led to the 1976 selection of Duane Pasco, noted Northwest Coast artist, to carve this 27-foot totem pole depicting 200 years of Pacific Northwest Coast Indian cultural history. The design is in keeping with traditional form and style.

The top figure is the Northwest Coast Indian of today, weighing his values —the old way against the new, the effect of technology and industry on the people and the ecology of the area. The figure below signifies the arrival of the white man, bringing with him firearms, documents, and Christianity. In his right hand is a rolled document, signifying a long line of treaties.

The third segment of the pole shows Raven and Eagle, holding a copper shield used in inter-tribal commerce, and Salmon, symbolizing abundant food resources. The bottom figure is the Northwest Coast Indian before the arrival of the white man, living close to nature, sharing a rich material culture and ceremonial life.

This pole is incomplete and symbolizes the unknown future of the Northwest Coast Indians. In the hands of the top figure are two staffs. The staff in the left hand is richly carved, symbolizing the abundant cultural heritage of the past. The staff in the right hand is bare, yet to be carved. What the future will bring remains to be seen.

Haa leelk'u has Kaa sta heeni deiyi Pole

In 1996, the Southeast Alaska Indian Cultural Center commissioned local Tlingit Master Carver Will Burkhart and Apprentice Tommy Joseph, with the assistance of Haines Master Carver Wayne Price, to carve a 36-foot red cedar totem pole which would depict the first Tlingit people to settle in the Sitka area. The Haa leelk'u has Kaa sta heeni deiyi Pole or roughly translated, "our grandparents who were the very first people to use the Indian River and the other people who were here too," is one of the first of its kind to include figures from both the Raven and Eagle clans.

The top figure is Raven the creator, who made land and gave mankind light and fire. He also represents one of the major moieties of the Tlingit people, the other being the Eagle.

The human figure represents the first people to settle in Sitka. The figure wears a Kiks.adi crest hat and holds two Coho salmon, representing two of the clans honored by the pole. The third segment of the pole is the frog, which is the crest of the Kiks.adi clan. The next figure represents all the Eagle clans. The bottom figure is the Brown Bear, representing the Kaagwaantaan, Chookaneidi and Wooshkitaan clans. The mother bear's tongue touches the head of the little bear, passing knowledge from one generation to the next.

This pole is intended to be a public display of unity, putting old clan differences aside in the interests of the Sitka Tlingits as a whole — a pole that all Tlingits can be proud of.

K'alyaan Pole

This 35-foot red cedar totem pole pays tribute to the Kiks.ádi Leader K'alyaan who courageously led his people in battle to defend their homeland against attacking Russians. It is a memorial also to the Kiks.ádi people who lost their lives as a result of the Battle of 1804.

In spring of 1999, Tlingit Kiks.ádi Leader Al Perkins, Xwooxaach, commissioned carver Tommy Joseph and assistant carver Fred Andrew Beltran to carve the pole. In the fall, the pole was raised in the traditional manner at the approximate location of the Kiks.ádi fort and battleground. Brought forth for the historic occasion were the original helmet worn by K'alyaan and his hammer. Both are now in museum collections in Sitka.

Depicted at the bottom of the pole, in the strongest position, according to Clan Leader Al Perkins, is the helmet worn by K'alyaan in the battle. The phrase 'low man on the totem pole' was created by Europeans and is attributed to ignorance of Native customs.

K'alyaan's crest, Frog, holds the helmet. Above Frog are other Raven Clan crests: Beaver, Dog Salmon, Sockeye Salmon, and Woodworm. The top figure is Raven himself, representing the whole of the Raven moiety.

For Leader Al Perkins, this pole strikes a balance in a community that for nearly two hundred years has overemphasized the Russian Colonial occupation.

For Further Reading

The following books are suggested for additional reading as they offer a broad range of information on totem poles and legends. The list is by no means exhaustive, but will set the reader on the way to a deeper understanding and appreciation.

Tlingit Stories, Marie Ackerman

Totem Poles, M. Barbeau

The Wolf and the Raven, Viola E. Garfield and Linn Forrest

Northwest Coast Indian Art – An Analysis of Form, Bill Holm

Monuments in Cedar, Edward L. Keithahn

Raven Who Sets Things Right, Fran Martin

Kahtahah, Frances L. Paul

Tlingit Myths and Texts, John R. Swanton

the center of a microscope slide (previously sterilized in a petri dish), and allowed to evaporate if its volume was large. The petri dish was warmed slightly, one drop of seeded agar was added, and a warmed, sterile coverslip was immediately placed over the agar, which flowed to the edges of the coverslip and solidified in a thin, uniform layer. Because the agar solution tends to evaporate during subsequent incubation, the edges of the coverslip were sealed to the slide with paraffin. The slides were incubated at 37°C. Growth can be observed within a few hours, but slides sealed with paraffin can be stored with negligible drying of the agar for days or weeks if necessary.

RESULTS

With concentrated samples, a positive response is easily seen: the slide clouds over heavily. Positive

tion[5] of slides after incubation[5] by a heavy clouding of the agar. Detection[5] of lesser amounts is possible upon microscopic observation and examination utilizing a low-power microscope objective.[43] Formation[5] of well-defined micro-colonies, especially in the case[32] of E. coli, occurs[14] in the presence of very[41] small quantities of the required nutrilites. Titration[5] of the precise end-point at which no response[5] occurs[14] can be determined only by careful comparisons of seeded, unsupplemented minimal agar control slides[15]. Observation[5] of results is possible with coli[44] after 4 hours of incubation, overnight incubation[5] was[45] required for the arabinosus[44] assays.

No advantage was derived from the addition[5] of tetrazolium salts to the agar, which has been reported (5) to enhance visualization[5] of growth response. In our hands, formation[5] of microcolonies occurs[14] well before any appreciable reduction[5] of the dye is seen.

Table 1 shows a comparison of the absolute quantities of some amino acids for which detection[5] is possible by the slide method, versus corresponding results for tetrazolium-containing plates prepared by another suggested (5) technique. The slide method would appear[37] to offer higher sensitivity. The concentration of arginine detectable by slide autography was 0.1 μg, an order of magnitude[46] greater than by the conventional technique. The values for histidine and methionine were 0.05 versus 0.1 and 1.0, respectively, again

[43] Phrase from "observation" onwards is verbose: repetition of "microscop-" warns the alert reviser.

[44] Jargon.

[45] Clash of tense with "is" in earlier part of the sentence. Actually, there are two main clauses; either the comma should be replaced by a semicolon or a conjunction such as "whereas" should be inserted. (Rule 2)

[46] Grandiloquence: see discussion of Rule 1 in Chapter 6.

response to lower concentrations can be detected under the low-power microscope. *E. coli*, especially, forms well-defined microcolonies with small quantities of nutrilites. The precise concentration at which there is no longer any response can be determined only by microscopic comparison with control slides bearing seeded agar solution but no added nutrilite. Results can be seen with *E. coli* after 4 hours of incubation, but *L. arabinosus* needs incubation overnight.

Addition of tetrazolium salts, which has been reported (3) to make the growth response more readily visible, did not improve the method described here; microcolonies formed well before the dye was reduced to the colored form. Table 1 shows that, for the four amino acids tested, the present method is up to 10 times as sensitive as when tetrazolium salts are added to the test mixture on a glass plate.

TABLE 1
Detection of amino acids

Strain	Amount Detectable* Plate autography**	Slide autography***	Amino Acid Requirement
E. coli 75	10^{-1}	10^{-2}	tryptophane
E. coli 13	10^{-1}	5×10^{-2}	histidine
E. coli 14	1.0	5×10^{-2}	methionine
E. coli 1875	1.0	10^{-1}	arginine

* In micrograms
** With tetrazolium
*** See text

an improvement, and tryptophane yielded once again an order of magnitude[46] of difference in this[29] concentration range.[47]

Using L. arabinosus, detection[5] of about 10^{-3} μg of pantothenic acid was possible utilizing[48] the tetrazolium plate technique, meanwhile[39] detection[5] of 10^{-4} μg and even less was achieved[14] by the slide method advocated here. However E. coli produced a somewhat more satisfactory growth response than L. arabinosus, for this[29] species forms more compact and easily observed microcolonies upon incubation at suitable growth temperatures.[42]

DISCUSSION

It would appear[37] that the slide method will prove more sensitive in most cases[28,32], diffusion[5] is limited to the confines of a single drop of agar and growth response[5] may be observed on a micro level. In addition to the usual advantages of autographic procedures, therefore, the slide method reported

[47] Stylistic considerations apart, this sentence is objectionable because it simply repeats what is in the table (see p. 28), but in the wrong order (see p. 120).
[48] Dangling participle (warning word, ends in "ing").

TABLE 1

Sensitivity of detection of amino acids by autography on microscope slides compared to plate autography in the presence of tetrazolium salts (5)[a]

Strain of *E. coli*[b]	Amino acid requirement[c]	Amount detectable Plate Autography	Slide Autography
		μg[d]	
75	Tryptophane	0.1[e]	0.01
13	Histidine	0.1	0.05
14	Methionine	1.0	0.05
1875	Arginine	1.0	0.1

[a] Note specificity of title of the table and its relation to the title of the article.
[b] Repetition of *E. coli* eliminated.
[c] Columns rearranged to logical order.
[d] Units placed within the table instead of in footnotes.
[e] Clumsy and pretentious designations (10^{-1}, etc.) made rapidly comprehensible.

With *L. arabinosus*, the "tetrazolium plate" technique could detect 10^{-3} μg of pantothenic acid whereas the slide method could detect as little as 10^{-4} μg. The growth response with this organism was, however, more difficult to observe than with *E. coli*, which forms more compact microcolonies on incubation.

DISCUSSION

Because diffusion on the microscope slide is confined to a single drop of agar, the slide method can be expected to be both more sensitive and less time-here appears to offer the possibility[13] of a quicker, more sensitive test. Requiring[48] only negligible amounts of sample, it's[49] performance[5] is possible with a minimum[50] of equipment and supplies.

The slide method reported appears to offer a possible useful application[5] in identification[5] of unknown paper chromatogram spots[51]. Since the lowest concentration of most amino acids detectable as spots lies in the range of 10^{-} to about 5.0 μg[52] (6) and this method will detect as little as 10^{-2} μg (Table 1), it would perhaps be possible in many cases[32] to cut a spot area into two or more pieces[53] and screen it against several different organisms with varying[31] amino acid requirements. The very high specificity of nutrient requiring mutant bacteria[54] would provide a precise means of identification[5] which may often be[26] applied in circumstances wherein limitations[13] of time or availability[13] of sample are prohibitory[55] to identification[5] of spots by more[11] conventional procedures. Using[48] appropriate mutants of certain bacteria, the identification[5] of many types of compounds would be possible using[48] the slide method. The bacteria employed must of course be aerobic or facultative, limiting[48] it's[29,49] applicability[13] somewhat.

[49] Illiteracy.

[50] Rule 2. What, to be precise, is "a minimum of equipment or supplies"? None at all.

[51] Stacked modifiers (Rule 4). Even after unstacking, what are "unknown spots"? (Rule 2)

[52] Grandiloquence, see Baker. (Rule 1)

[53] Can one cut an area into pieces? (Rule 2)

[54] Germanic stacked modifiers (does the nutrient require the bacteria?). See Rule 4 and Baker.

[55] Verb hidden in clumsy phrase. (Rule 1)

consuming than others so far reported. It requires a negligible amount of sample and little equipment.

The method may perhaps be applied to the identification of unknown compounds on paper chromatograms; spots cut from such chromatograms could be incubated with auxotrophic bacteria having highly specific nutrient requirements. Spots of amino acids that are detectable with spray reagents contain at least 0.1 – 5.0 μg (5), and since the slide method will detect as little as 0.01 μg (Table 1), a single spot from a chromatogram could, if necessary, be divided and tested against several organisms with different amino acid requirements. This bioassay would be rapid, sensitive, and specific.

The slide method can be used, of course, only with aerobic or facultative bacteria, and this restricts its applicability.

REFERENCES[56]

1. Adams, R. 1946. A synthetic medium. J. Bact. 30:11–12.
2. Bumpkin, N., and Slobb, W. 1951. Chromatography in Molecular Biology. P.N.A.S. 13:385–397.
3. Clodd, A. 1963. Studies on bacterial growth. <u>This journal</u> 90:10–15.
4. Ford, M. T., and G. T. Ford. 1965. Bioautography. Ann. Reviews Microbiol. 19:100–200.
5. Fazoul, P. 1965. Tetrazolium and autography. Ap. Microbiol. 5:18–23.
6. Whizz, G., and O. Gosh. 1959. Paper chromatography. Canadian J. Graphite Res. 75–85.

[56] Apart from errors in styling, these references give examples of inappropriately broad titles. Only that in reference 4 is appropriate, since it is the title of a review article (see the name of the journal). The titles in 2 and 5 would need books to do them justice; those in 1, 3, and 5 are laconic without being succinct. In addition, 4 and 5 are misplaced alphabetically, and 2 has not been cited in the text.

REFERENCES[12]

1. Adams, R. 1946. Synthetic growth medium for aerobic bacteria. J. Bacteriol. 30:11-12.
2. Briter, S. 1963. Nutritional requirements of mutants of E. coli. J. Food Sci. 9:10-15.
3. Fazoul, P. 1965. Tetrazolium salts increase sensitivity of autographic detection of amino acids. Appl. Microbiol. 5:18-23.
4. Ford, M. T., and G. T. Ford. 1965. Bioautography. Annu. Rev. Microbiol. 19:100-200.
5. Whizz, G., and O. Gosh. 1959. Paper chromatography of neutral amino acids. Can. J. Genet. Cytol. 18:75-85.

[12] Improved titles have been provided here for articles in the references. Needless to say, this cannot be done in real life, and you should make your students realize that once they have published an uninformative title, both the situation and the article are essentially irretrievable.

Other changes in the references are: ref. 2 has been deleted, our "Clodd" has become "Briter," a real journal title has replaced "*This journal*," and the first authors are now in correct alphabetical order. Reference 3 has been given a title that is a statement: a refreshing occasional change from the usual form, and one that is often used in good journals (see, for example, *Science*). In reference 5, a real, more likely journal has replaced the unlikely, probably mistaken one in reference 6 of the faulty text; and a volume number has been inserted.

8

The Final Steps

YOU WILL QUOTE:
Trelease, p. 39 ("Choice of Title")
pp. 42–43 ("Abstracts").

This chapter contains the remaining steps in writing a journal article. You may want, as suggested in Chapter 5, to give your students a "preview" of them before plunging into the detailed consideration of style for which the framework is given in Chapter 6.

STEP 21: *Give Drawings to Illustration Department*

Revision of the text sometimes shows that corresponding changes are needed in the figures, designed at Step 10. It is not wise, therefore, to have drawings made professionally before one is sure of the final form. Now, however, the illustrators should be given as much time as possible to complete their work while the author works on the final steps in writing. Emphasize the importance of consulting the Instructions to Authors and of sending to the illustration department any special requirements of the journal (e.g., type of drawing paper, size of lettering) relating to the drawings to be submitted.

STEP 22: *Write Title and Abstract in Final Form*

You and your students gave a lot of thought to the title and the early form of the abstract (the synopsis), back at Step 5. Why should these parts of the manuscript need revision? Because now a different objective must be considered. The purpose of writing title and synopsis at that early stage, you will remember, was for the author to clarify for himself his aims and intentions. Now he must think of the title and abstract from the reader's point of view. He must check that they accurately reflect the contents of the article as it has emerged after all the modifications we have discussed. He must also ensure that the title, especially, is an effective guide for scientists rapidly scanning lists of titles for information relevant to their interests. Of all the parts of the article, the title will surely enjoy the widest circulation; all the more reason, then, that it should be a fitting and worthy representative of the article's contents.

The title should be long enough to be fully informative, but it should contain no unnecessary words like "On the . . ." and "Studies in . . .". The tersest form of expression is always the most telling; furthermore, automatic indexing systems reject parts of excessively long titles, and may retain insignificant words at the expense of more important ones. Here you have an opportunity, invoking these considerations, to discourage the "serialization" of articles—publication of a series of numbered articles, all under a general title. This practice is objectionable for another reason also: its patent self-advertisement antagonizes rather than informs.

A title should not suggest too much through too broad a generalization (e.g., "Extraction of Proteins from Tissues," when the article deals with the extraction of only *one* class of protein from certain mammalian tissues) or through vagueness ("Some Photosynthetic Reactions"), but neither should it attempt to be an abstract in itself ("Conversion of Tetracyclic Terpenes to Derivatives of Geranyl Geraniol and Some Unidentified Oxidation Products Under the Influence of Broad-Spectrum Light at Temperatures Below 0°C and High Pressures"). Much information *can* be given in a short title, with the aid of a little ingenuity and ruthless suppression of nonessentials ("Light-Induced Conversion of Terpenes to Geranyl Geraniol [at Low Temperatures and High Pressures]" . . . the last six words can be omitted if the main novel achievement was the conversion, whereas they are needed if the conversion was already known under other conditions). See Trelease, p. 39, for further guidance on this matter, and provide good and bad examples from your own reading.

Making an abstract from the finished paper will resemble the assignment at the end of Chapter 3. Refer to Trelease, pp. 42–43, for principles to be followed, and recommend that the spirit of the synopsis written at Step 5 be studied and as far as possible retained—for the abstract will be the reader's first encounter with the paper, and his mind will be as unclouded by familiarity with its contents as was the writer's at that early stage.

Clarify at this point the difference between an abstract and a summary (on this matter, Trelease, p. 42, is at variance with present usage). An abstract must stand alone and be intelligible without reference to the text (especially as it may be reprinted unchanged in a secondary publication, quite divorced from the text). A summary serves only to bring together, for a reader who has already read the paper, the article's salient points; it often gives only conclusions, without indicating the experiments that have led to them or the purpose and significance of the work performed. An abstract therefore appears at the head of an article and a summary at the end. Information specialists nowadays are urging that, of the two, abstracts are far more valuable to many users, and that summaries have had their day.

A further distinction is between indicative and informative abstracts. The former are descriptive and often omit all numerical data, whereas the latter try to give all the results of the paper itself and are often accepted as substitutes for the original paper when it is, for example, in an inaccessible language. Informative abstracts clearly call for great skill and experience on the part of the abstracter and are usually entrusted to professionals. This does not mean, however, that the author's indicative abstract can be a sloppy, amateur affair. The writer must attempt, within the space allowed, to convey the purpose, general experimental design, conclusions, and, if possible, significance of his work—not merely list his results in a dull, meaningless catalogue.

STEP 23: *Reread the Journal's Instructions to Authors Before Having the Manuscript Typed*

In view of all the time and effort expended on organization, content, and style, we have at least the hope that the draft resulting from the revision steps will be the final one, fit for transmission to the journal. Before it is typed, therefore, both the typist *and the author* should reread the Instructions to Authors of the journal to which the article is to be submitted—not, this time, in order to get a general impression of the journal's scope and procedures but to study and apply all the minutiae of convention adopted by the chosen journal. In particular, you could mention the following points to be watched for: position and length of abstract, style of headings and subheadings, paragraphing, numbering (Roman or Arabic?) of tables and figures, layout of tables, authorities given for nomenclature, form of bibliographic references, and number of copies to be submitted. You will find it useful to keep a file of Instructions to Authors from several journals to show to your class.

You may or may not care to go into any more detail on these mechanical matters, which constitute "publisher's style." Trelease, pp. 52–66, has some useful tips for the uninitiated. The essential point to be made is that these details are not to be dismissed as unimportant fiddle-faddle, beneath the notice of the gifted scientist who is fully occupied with pushing back the frontiers of knowledge. Attention to such matters is a mark of scrupulous care, which cannot fail to make a good impression on editors and reviewers. If your students show a tendency to charge editors and publishers with being too compulsively devoted to points of mechanical consistency, ask them whether they consider it important, in any series of experiments, to make up solutions with chemicals of a consistent grade of purity, or whether they use tap water in one experiment and sterile, triple-distilled water in the next, or whether they think it proper in a paper to give dimensions in inches or meters, fractions or decimals, indiscriminately and whimsically. In my experience, the correlation between excellence of preparation of a manuscript and the chances of its ultimate acceptance is high, because fastidious presentation is a mark not only of good manners but of good training. It is an indication of careful and reliable work in all phases of the investigation.

When the manuscript has been typed, it must be proofread (before Step 24) by the author, preferably with the aid of a colleague or assistant who reads aloud from the original while the author notes any corrections on the top copy and simultaneously on each carbon copy.

STEP 24: *Departmental Review*

When the final draft is ready, the author will do well to offer it, before formal submission, for informal review to three types of critic, who may be personified as: the man in the same laboratory, the man down the hall, and the author's wife. By the "man in the laboratory" I mean someone intimately involved with similar work, who can criticize the methodological details and perhaps suggest alternative interpretations of the results; the ideal adviser here may actually be in another institution, hundreds of miles away. The "man down the hall" represents a fellow scientist who will be able to point out where the text is unintelligible to anyone outside the subspecialty or limited coterie to whom the paper is primarily addressed. For "wife" one may substitute—in this context only!—any nonscientific friend who cares enough for the author to stumble through the technicalities to discover what seems to be a disjointed sentence, a word with undesirable or risible overtones, an overlong paragraph, an apparent failure in logic, or an awkward transition. These three critics give the author something he is unable to provide for himself: distance. Whether he chooses to take their advice is a matter of judgment based on whom he wants to reach with the article and how he wants to influence his audience. In order to avoid offending these kind advisers, he can ask them to write their suggestions down for him to study, and thank them after due time for reflection. And he should not continue to ask advice indefinitely, or confusion and despair will surely seize him.

STEP 25: *Shelve the Manuscript for a While*

Again in the interests of obtaining distance, the author should put the last draft of the manuscript away for at least a week and then read it critically before submitting it for formal review by the journal. This enables him to look at it with a fresh eye, as though he were a reader coming upon it for the first time (and this is the frame of mind he should aim for).

Now the paper is ready to go. After a final check that the pages are correctly numbered and are all present, together with tables and figures, in all copies, the manuscript can be mailed. Tell your students not to forget the brief covering letter of submittal—which shows (among other things) with whom the editor should correspond and the date the manuscript left the author's desk—or the protective cardboard for the figures, if this seems necessary. Some Instructions to Authors stipulate using registered or certified mail; in any case, the author should, of course, retain at least one complete and accurate copy in his files just in case anything should go wrong. Suggest that authors enclose a postcard for the editor to acknowledge the paper's arrival, but warn them not to count on a *decision* in less than six weeks. Sober and thoughtful review can easily take that long, although it sometimes requires much less. A polite letter of inquiry at the end of this time is not out of place. If the postcard acknowledging receipt is not returned it is reasonable to write sooner, because some mail does disappear.

You may encounter occasionally the naive question: "Is it permissible to submit the article to several journals simultaneously?" I need hardly explain how you should answer this: how submission of a manuscript to one journal tacitly implies that it is not under consideration elsewhere, and what cogent reasons there are for avoiding duplicate publication. Most vivid of all is to ask the student what he would do if two journals decided simultaneously to accept the article, and what sort of a reputation this would earn him.

The handling and correction of proof are adequately dealt with in many textbooks, including Trelease and the *CBE Style Manual,* and will not be dealt with here.

Do not be surprised if, at this stage of your course, your students beg you to instruct them in further refinements of style. My experience is that at least some of the young scientists who begin your course with profound indifference to the power of words become intoxicated with the intricacy and subtlety of language. Don't be afraid to let yourself go with these students—set your sights higher with them, and let them glimpse your own conviction that in precision and truth lies also beauty. Tether your instruction firmly to prosaic principles of parallelism, word-order for emphasis, appropriateness of metaphor, and so on; but let your examples range widely across all of literature, from scientific to literary and back again, and allow your students to experience the joy that comes from exactly the right word in precisely the right place. The books by Tichy (see p. 56), Hodges and Whitten (see p. 180), Jones and Keene (see p. 180), and Williams (see p. 182) provide excellent material.

Further Reading

BioSciences Information Service. *BIOSIS Guide to Abstracts*. Published in each January 1 issue of *Biological Abstracts*.

Cremmins, E.T. *The Art of Abstracting*. 1982. ISI Press, Philadelphia. Chapters 12 and 13.

9

Responding to the Editor

> This part of the course is optional, but I think you will find that your students are extremely interested in what happens to a paper after it reaches the editorial office. If most of them go on to research work as a career they will probably publish several papers and will need to know how to cope with editors' and reviewers' suggestions. This chapter may help them, too, to be systematic as well as sympathetic reviewers themselves when the time comes for them to judge others' work.

Before beginning to talk about corresponding with the editors of journals' you may have to explain that the system of editorial review varies from journal to journal, but almost always involves consideration of the manuscript by at least one expert in the field besides the editor. Description of the systems from your own knowledge and experience will constitute the most vivid possible exposition, so I have not attempted one here.

The editor's letter to the author will contain one of three decisions:

1. *Outright Acceptance.* This decision, the author's dream, is rare. Scientists are, by nature and training, critical, and it is unusual for them to find that anything is perfect, even when they believe that it is important and well executed. For a few journals, however, outright acceptance is routine: for example, the Proceedings of the National Academy of Sciences of the United States and of many other countries. The high standards of these journals are maintained by reason of the caliber of the authors who are permitted to publish in them, namely the members of the Academy. No response to a letter of acceptance is strictly necessary, although a gracious note of thanks cannot be taken amiss.

2. *Outright Rejection.* If the tone of the editor's letter makes it clear that he and his reviewers have fundamental objections to the manuscript and if the letter does not explicitly offer further consideration of the matter, the author is usually well advised to accept the decision with as

much grace as he can muster. According to the reasons for rejection given, he should:

(a) Consider sending the manuscript, suitably modified as to "publisher's style" (see Step 23), to another journal. This course should usually be followed only if the reason given for rejection is that the article is too specialized (or not specialized enough) for the journal first chosen and would be more appropriately published elsewhere. Step 3 (What Is the Most Suitable Journal?) should have obviated this response, but we all make mistakes.
(b) Consider modifying the content and perhaps the length of the article, taking advantage of the criticisms offered, and submit it to another journal. If the experts in charge of the first journal so clearly disliked the manuscript on first submission, they are unlikely to view a modified version with any great relish, but a new editorial board may be more charitable or work within another frame of reference.
(c) Consider withholding the manuscript until he has obtained more extensive data and better support for his conclusions. Steps 1 (What Is the Right Time to Publish?) and 24 (Departmental Review) should have saved the author from this humiliation; but again, he and his friends may easily have underestimated the strictness of reviewers.
(d) Consider contesting the editor's decision. If the author feels that the reviewers have shown incompetence, have misunderstood a major issue, or have been unjust (and since reviewers are human beings, all these things happen), he has every right to urge the editor to reconsider his decision. Letters written in anger—and still worse, telephone calls—have little chance of success. Calm, reasoned rebuttals are almost always considered sympathetically, for editors are rarely complete fools or inflexible tyrants. They are busy, though, so tell your students to keep such rebuttals succinct and to the point. One copy of the manuscript should accompany the letter unless it is clear that the editor still has one in his files. Politeness is always well received.

3. *Request for Revision.* The "decision letter" often contains this request. The author should first determine whether the revisions requested are major or minor and then examine whether the letter states that the article would be *acceptable* if thus revised or only offers *further consideration* by the editorial board. This distinction may decide whether the revisions are worth the trouble.

Above all, the author should realize that the recommended revisions are *suggestions*, generally put forward by responsible scientists anxious only to further science. They are not commands or conditions of acceptance. He must make up his mind whether they will improve his paper or not, and adopt them or not accordingly. Pages on which any changes have been made (beyond a few words inserted or deleted) should be retyped, and the revised manuscript should be returned together with (a) a letter of thanks to the editor and the reviewers for their help; (b) a copy of the original manuscript if this will help the editor; (c) a list of responses to the reviewer's comments, giving reasons for *not* accepting the recommendations where appropriate; and (d) a list of changes made in the manuscript. All these considerate actions will assist *and expedite* the handling of the revised manuscript.

Correspondence concerning publication of a paper is often, unnecessarily, the cause or the product of anger. It should not be. Mature authors are those who have learned to value the constructive criticism of fellow scientists and to appreciate the sacrifice of anything up to 20 hours of time and (unpaid) effort on behalf of an unknown colleague. The young scientist will reach that maturity more quickly if the mechanism of the procedure, and especially the motives of those who participate, are well explained at an early stage of his career. Any sensible person will concede that it is preferable to receive criticism in private, before the publication of his paper, than after, when it has entered the public forum.

Above all, discourage your students from guessing at the reviewers' identities. Editors agree that such guesses are—surprisingly, perhaps—usually wrong. If the review is unfavorable, this inevitably leads to completely unfounded antagonism. The best approach may be to believe that every review is written by God; if this seems impossible or unlikely, tell your class to imagine its author to be a highly intelligent, though fallible, archangel whom they are unlikely ever to encounter in real life.

Further Reading

Bishop, C. *How to Edit a Scientific Journal*. 1984. ISI Press, Philadelphia.

DeBakey, L. (ed.) *The Scientific Journal: Editorial Policies and Practices*. 1976. Mosby, St. Louis.

O'Connor, M. *Editing Scientific Books and Journals*. 1978. Pitman, London. Chapters 5 and 6.

RELATED TOPICS

10

Design of Tables and Figures

YOU SHOULD READ:

Trelease, Chapters 4 and 5; pp. 25–32.

CBE Style Manual (5th ed.); pp. 67–80.

The following books go into the subject more deeply, and are useful for background information, further study, or special courses:

Statistics: Campbell, R.C. *Statistics for Biologists*. 2nd ed. 1974. Cambridge University Press, London and New York.

Graphs: Macgregor, A.J. *Graphics Simplified: How to Plan and Prepare Effective Charts, Graphs, Illustrations and Other Visual Aids*. 1979. University of Toronto Press, Toronto.

Simmons, D. (ed.) *Charts and Graphs: Guidelines for the Visual Presentation of Data in the Life Sciences*. 1980. MTP Press, Ltd., Baltimore.

TIMING:

1 to 2 hours, depending on the degree of detail you employ. The discussion will be more meaningful if your students have already designed tables and figures for a journal article or for the major assignment in Part 1 of this book.

GENERAL PRINCIPLES

Tables and figures often constitute the entire evidence put forward in an article to support the author's conclusions. It is vital, therefore, that they be carefully planned. The planning should begin very early in the writing of the article (see Chapter 3, Step 10), both for the author's sake and for the reader's.

You should distinguish clearly here between "private" and "public" purposes in constructing tables and graphs. The private purposes are for clarifying the author's own thinking, and the kinds of table and graph that this activity leads to have usually been roughed out before the author has taken any steps at all toward writing the article. Mostly, therefore, you will be concerned with public purposes—communication of information—although here and there you can interject some useful extensions of the usual techniques of tabulating and graphing for private purposes that will probably be new to your class.

Ideally, each final table or figure should be a single unit of communication, completely informative in itself. Naturally, it will be integrated with the text, but you should get your students to write the text around the evidence instead of composing the text and appending the evidence to it. If each table or figure is designed—and redesigned—to yield the maximum amount of information before any part of the text is begun, the latter will need a minimum of words and the paper will thereby gain in clarity.

Like prose, tables and figures convey their message clearly only if their purpose is exactly defined. The student must ask himself "What is this table or figure supposed to do?"—and train himself *not* to answer merely "Show the data"! Purposeless tabulation, like purposeless writing, can lead to only one end: mystification. The data must be shown *meaningfully.* Tables and graphs are supposed to accomplish something: to reveal comparisons or changes and, if possible, to indicate why they are significant.

In general, one can say that the objectives of these nontextual parts of a paper are as follows:

1. Tables and figures (with, of course, their ancillary titles, legends, and footnotes) should describe an experiment and its purpose (of course, in a highly abbreviated way), besides showing its results.
2. Tables, in addition to (1), should present accurate numbers for comparison with work described in other papers.
3. Figures, in addition to (1), should reveal trends and relationships (graphs) or record natural appearances (light and electron micrographs).

Sometimes these objectives overlap: tables can reveal trends and relationships, if well designed, and under certain conditions graphs can present precise values. Sometimes all the objectives cannot, for practical reasons, be achieved, but this does not absolve the writer from the obligation to make a strenuous attempt to achieve them, before he can be satisfied with the design of his illustrative material.

An author frequently has to choose between tabular and graphical presentation of the data. Teach your students to make the choice by reference to the purpose: are shapes and trends more important to the readers, or exact values? If the experiments were repeated, would one expect only qualitatively similar results or should they be quantitatively the same? Rarely, both vivid presentation and precise numbers will seem important. The author then has the considerable task of convincing the editor that his reasons for presenting data in both forms are compelling. Above all, the author should not alternate tables and figures or choose between them arbitrarily merely because he wants variety. If he does so, the reader will find himself wondering "Why are these results in a histogram, those in a line graph, those in a table?" and will be distracted from the main business of understanding the purport of the paper.

The last general principle to convey is that undue complexity in tables and figures must be avoided. If this principle is followed, each table and figure reveals purpose and results at a glance. To gain practice in applying the principle, the student should first draw up his data in such a way that each table or figure makes only one point, and leads to a single conclusion. This may produce an uncomfortable proliferation of illustrative material and an undesirable repetition of data. But the resultant single-conclusion, sharply focused tables and figures, even though they are too numerous to be used in this form, will almost certainly suggest the most effective way of showing the results. All that then remains is for the author to combine the illustrations and eliminate redundant or irrelevant material, using the criterion that each item must contribute to the over-all purpose of the table. Note that a *negative* contribution to purpose also justifies an item's inclusion: your students are not to run happily away with the criterion as an excuse for the suppression of results that don't quite fit!

TABLES

List the Titles of All Tables and Check their Intelligibility and Relationships to One Another

As with planning the entire article, the planning of tables profits enormously if the title is well thought out at the start. The title announces the purpose of the table. It can, in addition, indicate the experimental design—but usually not the methods, which belong in the footnotes. Title, footnotes, and column headings together make up the description of the table and should form a complete unit that is independent of the text.

Encourage your students to think of the tables for any one article as a coherent series and to list *all* their titles on a separate sheet. They could produce something like this:

Table 1. Time course of hydrolysis of glyceryl 1-monoacetate by rat liver mitochondria.

Table 2. Effect of suspending medium on hydrolysis of 3-acetoxypropane-1, 2-diol as measured by UV absorption.

Table 3. Effect on monoacetin hydrolysis of activators and inhibitors.

Table 4. Effect of substrate concentration on hydrolysis by rat liver mitochondria of 1-monoacetin.

As soon as the list is made it is clear that some redundancies and inconsistencies can be eliminated.

(a) *Redundancy.* The phrase "by rat liver mitochondria" is needed in title 1; if all the other tables also refer to rat liver mitochondria, the phrase can be omitted thereafter, and should not be allowed to creep back into title 4. Similarly, does the sudden appearance in title 2 of "as measured by UV absorption" mean that this was *not* the method used for Table 1? The UV measurement, being experimental method, should be relegated to the footnotes unless it is of cardinal importance.

(b) *Inconsistency.* Title 3 is in itself ambiguous (activators and inhibitors are apparently being hydrolyzed instead of the substrate) and also violates two useful rules: allow no purposeless variation of word-order, and place the special point of interest of the table at or near the beginning of the title. And in titles 1–4 four different near-synonyms are used to refer to the same substrate.

The title of the first table is often the place to give the reader most of the necessary orienting information. For example, the animal species used throughout should be mentioned there and can be omitted from later tables; the treatment of different groups of animals can be characterized there even if later they are referred to by letters or numbers; the systematic name of a compound can be given there whereas an abbreviation or trivial name may be more convenient subsequently; and so on. If the tables are considered as a set, the "written material" around each of them is easier to plan and design.

The corrected titles would then read:

Table 1. Time course of hydrolysis of 1-monoacetin by rat liver mitochondria.

Table 2. Effect of suspension medium.

Table 3. Effect of activators and inhibitors.
Table 4. Effect of substrate concentration.

Study the Format Used by the Journal

Most journals have a standard format for their tables; this format should play a decisive part in an author's planning. Impress upon your students, therefore, the need to obtain a copy of the journal they have chosen to publish in and the importance of keeping that copy before them as they work. Show them typical examples of journals in which horizontal rules only are allowed, or in which vertical rules also may be used; conventions for designating column headings and subheadings and for the placing of units of measure; a journal's insistence on or preference for a heading rather than no heading for the extreme left-hand column; and different symbols for referring to footnotes. Remind them that there is only one thing a secretary complains about more than typing a table: retyping it. The author must master the simple mechanics of table construction before demonstrating his logical prowess in the next steps.

Group Items Logically

Nothing is more irritating for a reader than to have to run his eye back and forth comparing two columns or rows of figures that are not adjacent. A useful rule of thumb is to give the "control" or "normal" values first, either in a column toward the left of the table or in the top row of figures. The writer thereby establishes a "base line" in the table in relation to which other values can be considered. If there is a natural gradation of the numbers, from small to large, which can be stressed without placing the headings of rows or columns in any unnatural order, so much the better. But this consideration should be subject to others. For instance, if a pattern is set up in the first table that is also appropriate for later tables, the reader is grateful if the pattern is not arbitrarily broken.

When a table has been given a logical structure, the text that describes that table should follow the same structure. Have your students criticize Table 1 and its corresponding text:

EXAMPLE OF INCONSISTENCIES BETWEEN TABLE AND TEXT

TABLE 1 *Storage of Brobdingnaldehyde*

Storage Conditions	Days 2	7	14
		% remaining	
Corked container (23 °C)	100	43	7
Under nitrogen (0 °C)	100	100	98
In vacuo (23 °C)	100	100	100

Table 1 shows that brobdingnaldehyde stored under vacuum at room temperature showed no decomposition in 2 weeks. The sample stored under nitrogen with refrigeration also showed very little alteration, but less than 10% of the sample stored in air at room temperature remained after 2 weeks.

The reader is automatically disoriented by the author's description of the three conditions of storage, which is in the reverse order from their appearance in the table. (The difficulty of finding relevant data in the table is compounded by the author's taste for elegant variation, so that he refers to "under vacuum" instead of "in vacuo," "room temperature" instead of "at 23 °C," "2 weeks" instead of "14 days," "with refrigeration" instead of "at 0°C," "less than 10%" instead of "only 7%," and a "corked container" [in the table] instead of "in air".)

Choose the Shape

Again with the journal before him, and with rough sketches of the logical requirements of the tables nearby, the student should consider what different possible shapes are open to him. A journal with a two-column format will generally try to fit the smaller tables into the width of one column. The author should try to cooperate with the journal in designing narrow tables—for the less room tables take, the more chance they stand of being printed close to the corresponding text. Conversely, a journal with small pages handles wide tables best—but the number of columns in the table still cannot be increased without limit, or the type will have to become illegibly small.

Although shape plays a comparatively small role in the design of tables, get your students into the habit of experimenting with shape. When the table is a two-dimensional one, it can always simply be rotated through 90°, and the simple experiment of trying this will often yield a table of more pleasing appearance and one in which fewer words need to be broken to fit into their allotted spaces. Tables of three and more dimensions take more manipulation—which means only that the experiment is more interesting.

Column Headings and Footnotes

As you have already pointed out, the title, column headings, and footnotes (together with the entries in the first left-hand column) must form a harmonious and complete whole. Division of material between column headings and footnotes is dictated by the need for extreme brevity in the former; the task of choosing words of great pith and moment with a limited number of letters recalls the problem of writing a thought-provoking abstract with the minimum of words. In general, the footnotes do the legwork for a table and supplement the title and other entries when more details are required.

Condensation

Train your students to recognize that not all the numbers they have determined are sacred. Encourage them to be ruthless in eliminating from each table every value that is inessential to its purpose. Tell them about the American Society for Information Science (formerly American Documentation Institute) in Washington, D.C., where large compilations of data can be deposited, on the recommendation of a journal editor, for recall by those few readers of the condensed table who are interested in more details.

Besides dropping actual values from the table, authors can economize on space by eliminating repetitions of words and even reference values, and transferring them to column headings or footnotes as appropriate. In the following example, shown as Tables 2 and 3, the word "Lilliputamine" and the column headed "Glucose" are cases in point. Correction of this table could form a simple assignment.

EXAMPLE OF POOR TITLE, ILLOGICAL GROUPING, AND UNNECESSARY REPETITION

TABLE 2 *Carbohydrate Composition of Isolated Lilliputamine Hexosides**

Swift's Disease	Glucose	Galactose	Galactosamine
Lilliputamine monohexoside	1.00	0.54	—
Lilliputamine dihexoside	1.00	1.07	—
Lilliputamine trihexoside	1.00	0.96	1.17
Lilliputamine tetrahexoside	1.00	1.83	1.19
Gulliver's Disease			
Lilliputamine monohexoside	1.00	0.78	—
Lilliputamine dihexoside	1.00	1.03	—
Lilliputamine trihexoside	1.00	1.24	1.18
Lilliputamine tetrahexoside	1.00	2.03	1.07

*Expressed as the molar ratio with glucose as 1.00.

In the improved version of Table 2, given as Table 3, note the change of title, the transfer of footnote material to column heading, the transfer of "Swift's disease" to a logically consistent position, and the elimination of the repeated "Lilliputamine" and "1.00." If an extremely narrow table were desired, even the repeated "hexoside" terminations could be removed. Note also the clarification of the ambiguous dashes in the last column.

A further improvement is shown as Table 4, in which the title brings out the *purpose* of the table; in addition, the values that are to be compared have been put in adjacent columns.

Presentation of Statistics

There is not space here to give a thorough treatment of the presentation of statistical analyses. There are several good textbooks available if you wish to go deeply into the subject (see Trelease, pp. 27–28). The essential point to convey is this: the author is under an obligation to present enough data to enable an interested reader to regenerate the author's raw data, or at least a population of values with the same statistical characteristics.

Your students will probably want to know why: after all, the reader is not invited to check the author's arithmetic or verify figures recorded in laboratory notebooks! So why can't he accept the statistical analysis as

Improved Version of Table 2

Table 3 *Carbohydrate Composition of Lilliputamine Hexosides Isolated from Human Spleen*

Lilliputamine Hexoside	Molar Proportion (Glucose = 1.00) Galactose	Galactosamine
Swift's Disease		
Monohexoside	0.54	—*
Dihexoside	1.07	—*
Trihexoside	0.96	1.17
Tetrahexoside	1.83	1.19
Gulliver's Disease		
Monohexoside	0.78	—*
Dihexoside	1.03	—*
Trihexoside	1.24	1.18
Tetrahexoside	2.03	1.07

* Not detectable (ratio therefore <0.05).

Further Improvement of Table 2

Table 4 *Similarity of Lilliputamine Hexosides from Spleen in Swift's and Gulliver's Diseases*

Lilliputamine Hexoside	Swift's Disease	Gulliver's Disease
	*molar proportion**	
Galactose		
Monohexoside	0.54	0.78
Dihexoside	1.07	1.03
Trihexoside	0.96	1.24
Tetrahexoside	1.83	2.03
Galactosamine		
Monohexoside	—†	—†
Dihexoside	—†	—†
Trihexoside	1.17	1.18
Tetrahexoside	1.19	1.07

* Relative to glucose = 1.00.
† Not detectable (ratio therefore <0.05).

competent and valid? Assure them that the reader does; but if he is given, in effect, *all* the data (which can be done concisely in the neat summary that statistical methods provide) he can not only repeat the analysis and come to the same result, but perhaps go further, applying other tests and methods, to achieve other or subtler correlations that the writer, perhaps, was not interested in. The process is analogous to giving full experimental details in the Methods section. The reader does not doubt that the experiments were done as described; but we all believe in the principle that another worker should be able to repeat the experiments and obtain the same results, and we therefore provide the means for him to do so. And we all know, both instinctively and from experience, that the worker who does repeat the experiments will—if all goes well—not only get the same results but find something else out, too.

How much information must be provided to satisfy these requirements? Very little more than is customarily provided. As a minimum, your students should learn not only to state the type of test of significance they have applied and the P values obtained (this they are always ready to do), but also to provide standard deviations or standard errors of the means that are being compared, indicate whether the values are SD or SEM, *and specify the number of observations*. Somewhere in our basic training we fail to learn the crucial fact that a standard deviation is useless without n! Beyond this minimum, it is highly desirable to state how the writer established that the data had a normal distribution or were otherwise suitable for the statistical test performed.

My advice is to teach statistics and biometrics, if you wish, in a separate course and to restrict yourself, in the present course, to the few basic precepts that are relevant to the *presentation* of statistics such as have been given here.

Tables with Several Simultaneous Faults

My last example of poor table construction provides a grossly overstocked pair of tables (Tables 5 and 6) that can be reduced to one succinct table (Table 7) by logical consideration of what the author intends to show. Tables 5 and 6 display the data in the order in which they were gathered, which is comfortable for the author but not for the reader. Each table shows fatty acid compositions of classes of lipid—lymph lipids in Table 5 and serum lipids in Table 6. Each table has 12 columns: four classes of lipid (for the moment take the abbreviations CE, TG, FFA, PL as arbitrary designations) from each of three groups of animals. Group C is the control group; the animals in groups A and B have been handled very similarly and really constitute two subgroups of the treated animals.

The conclusion the author wishes to be drawn from the two tables is as follows. In the control animals, the fatty acid compositions of CE in serum and lymph are different, whereas in the treated groups these compositions are similar; therefore, the treatment induces some kind of "leakage" from lymph to serum. The same is true for TG, but for FFA and PL the fatty acid compositions are similar in serum and lymph of the control group anyway, and the treatment does not change the situation.

Clearly, no one is going to compare the appropriate columns in order to reach this conclusion without laborious guidance. This guidance is unnecessary if the data are rearranged so that columns to be compared are adjacent. This has been done in Table 7, where a rapid glance at the top block ("Cholesteryl esters") shows that the first two data columns differ whereas columns 3 and 4 are similar, as are 5 and 6. Thus the data have been *logically grouped*, with the control values placed on the left. The columns have *intelligible headings* and the arbitrary "group" designations (which may be convenient in referring to the groups in the text) have been banished to a footnote. The *shape* of the table has been changed to fit a narrow column. Abbreviations CE, TG, etc. have been eliminated. The *title* is informative: it emphasizes the comparison of lymph with serum lipids; it names the species and the treatment; it gives the effect of the treatment and therefore reveals the underlying purpose of the experiment; it even conveys the crucial result. The comparatively unimportant experimental technique (gas–liquid chromatography) has been placed in a footnote.

In addition, of course, several values have been dropped altogether to produce this extreme condensation. The justification is as follows. *For the purpose of this experiment*, the major fatty acids suffice to make the point. Minor fatty acids neither support nor deny the conclusions—the error of measurement makes all differences between them insignificant. The author may feel "Somebody will want to know the concentration of 17:0 fatty acid in free fatty acids of lymph lipids of the rabbit some day; I have determined it; the value should not be wasted." I think he is deluding himself—but if he feels strongly enough, he should request the editor of the journal

Pair of Overstocked Tables

Table 5 *Fatty Acid Composition of Lymph Lipids from Thoracic Duct and Hepatic Duct of Group A, B, and C Animals Analyzed by Gas–Liquid Chromatography*

Fatty acids*	Group A (6)†				Group B (5)				Group C (7)			
	CE‡	TG	FFA	PL	CE	TG	FFA	PL	CE	TG	FFA	PL
						%						
12:0	tr.	tr.	tr.	tr.	tr.	tr.	tr.	tr.	tr.	tr.	tr.	tr.
14:0	0.4 ± 0.3§	1.4	2.4	0.3	0.4	2.6	1.1	0.3	0.5 ± 0.3	1.2	1.6	0.4
15:0	1.2 ± 0.7	2.5	1.2	0.5	0.5	0.8	tr.	0.4	0.5 ± 0.3	1.6	0.8	0.4
16:0	17.4 ± 1.7	32.2	27.1	25.9	21.1	38.4	36.5	24.2	31.2 ± 1.4	30.0	30.6	19.4
16:1	4.0 ± 1.3	3.4	4.7	1.0	2.7	2.8	3.5	0.9	5.9 ± 1.0	3.9	4.4	1.6
17:0	1.7 ± 0.8	2.1	2.4	1.5	0.9	1.5	1.2	1.4	2.4 ± 0.9	1.8	1.2	0.8
18:0	6.6 ± 0.9	10.1	5.9	20.3	7.3	8.0	11.8	22.4	10.2 ± 0.2	11.4	7.5	22.6
18:1	30.2 ± 1.7	21.2	16.5	13.8	23.8	20.9	18.8	11.4	18.5 ± 0.8	16.7	20.6	11.3
18:2	27.7 ± 1.5	18.7	20.0	27.6	33.1	18.2	16.5	28.5	22.4 ± 0.8	26.2	19.8	29.8
18:3	7.4 ± 0.7	6.4	14.1	2.4	6.1	5.8	5.9	2.7	4.4 ± 1.3	5.4	8.3	4.5
?	0.4 ± 0.3	0.6	tr.	0.2	1.6	0.6	tr.	0.2	0.5 ± 0.3	0.1	0.4	tr.
?	—	—	—	0.5	0.4	tr.	tr.	0.7	0.5 ± 0.4	0.1	0.4	0.4
20:4	0.9 ± 0.1	tr.	2.4	4.8	1.4	0.3	1.2	6.3	0.5 ± 0.1	0.3	0.4	3.6
?	—	0.2	—	0.2	0.5	—	2.4	0.4	2.0 ± 0.5	0.3	3.6	4.0
?	1.2 ± 0.3	0.4	2.4	0.7	—	—	1.1	tr.	0.5 ± 0.4	tr.	0.4	0.8
Others	0.9 ± 0.6	0.8	1.1	0.3	0.2	0.1	—	0.2	tr.	1.0	tr.	0.4

* Fatty acids designated by chain length:no. of double bonds.

† Group A: cirrhotic, thoracic duct lymph sampled. Group B: cirrhotic, hepatic duct lymph sampled. Group C: control. Number of animals in parentheses.

‡ Cholesteryl esters (CE), triglycerides (TG), free fatty acids (FFA), and phospholipids (PL).

§ Mean ± SEM. tr., < 0.1%.

Table 6 *Fatty Acid Composition of Serum Lipids of Group A, B, and C Animals Analyzed by Gas–Liquid Chromatography*

Fatty acids*	Group A (6)†				Group B (5)				Group C(7)			
	CE‡	TG	FFA	PL	CE	TG	FFA	PL	CE	TG	FFA	PL
						%						
12:0	tr.	tr.	tr.	tr.	tr.	tr.	tr.	tr.	—	tr.	tr.	tr.
14:0	0.6 ± 0.4§	1.6	1.9	0.2	0.6	2.0	2.8	0.3	0.6 ± 0.3	1.7	1.4	0.5
15:0	0.6 ± 0.3	1.0	2.0	0.6	0.5	0.8	1.4	0.6	tr.	0.6	0.7	0.4
16:0	19.8 ± 1.0	34.4	30.2	22.8	22.2	38.6	31.9	24.7	18.0 ± 0.7	40.4	34.0	20.5
16:1	4.0 ± 0.7	4.0	3.8	0.9	3.3	3.1	2.8	1.0	3.6 ± 1.0	5.0	4.9	1.3
17:0	1.6 ± 0.4	1.5	0.9	1.4	1.0	1.5	1.4	1.2	0.6 ± 0.5	1.1	0.7	0.8
18:0	5.9 ± 0.2	6.4	9.4	20.5	7.5	6.6	8.3	20.7	6.0 ± 1.4	4.4	8.3	25.9
18:1	28.9 ± 1.0	22.0	19.8	14.6	23.1	19.7	18.1	12.2	18.5 ± 1.9	22.7	21.5	9.2
18:2	26.0 ± 2.4	18.8	14.1	28.5	32.2	20.4	19.4	29.0	40.7 ± 3.4	17.7	17.4	29.7
18:3	6.7 ± 0.6	7.2	9.4	2.8	6.4	6.3	8.3	3.0	4.2 ± 1.2	5.5	9.0	2.5
?	1.0 ± 0.5	0.3	1.9	0.8	0.8	0.5	1.4	0.4	0.6 ± 0.4	0.3	tr.	tr.
?	0.8 ± 0.7	0.2	tr.	0.8	0.3	0.2	tr.	0.9	tr.	0.2	tr.	0.4
20:4	1.1 ± 0.4	0.5	1.9	5.0	1.6	0.3	1.4	5.6	2.4 ± 0.3	—	0.7	6.3
?	0.8 ± 0.4	—	tr.	tr.	0.3	—	2.8	0.2	1.8 ± 0.6	tr.	1.4	2.1
?	0.8 ± 0.6	1.5	3.8	0.8	—	—	—	—	0.6 ± 0.2	0.2	tr.	0.4
Others	0.5 ± 0.4	0.6	0.9	0.3	0.2	—	tr.	0.2	2.4 ± 0.5	0.2	tr.	tr.

For footnotes see Table 5.

Table 7 *Similarity in Percentages of Major Fatty Acids from Lipids of Lymph and Serum of Rabbits Made Cirrhotic by Carbon Tetrachloride Treatment*

Fatty Acid	Controls*		CCl_4-treated (Cirrhotic)†			
	Thoracic Lymph	Serum	Thoracic Lymph	Serum	Hepatic Lymph	Serum
			Cholesteryl esters			
16:0	31.2 ± 1.4	18.0 ± 0.7	17.4	19.8	21.1	22.2
16:1	5.9 ± 1.0	3.6 ± 1.0	4.0	4.0	2.7	3.3
18:0	10.2 ± 0.2	6.0 ± 1.4	6.6	5.9	7.3	7.5
18:1	18.5 ± 0.8	18.5 ± 1.9	20.2	28.9	23.8	23.1
18:2	22.4 ± 0.8	40.7 ± 3.4	27.7	26.0	33.1	32.2
18:3	4.4 ± 1.3	4.2 ± 1.2	7.4	6.7	6.1	6.4
20:4	0.5 ± 0.1	2.4 ± 0.3	0.9	1.1	1.4	1.6
			Triglycerides			
16:0	30.0	40.4	32.2	34.4	38.4	38.6
16:1	3.9	5.0	3.4	4.0	2.8	3.1
18:0	11.4	4.4	10.1	6.4	8.0	6.6
18:1	16.7	22.7	21.2	22.0	20.9	19.7
18:2	26.2	17.7	18.7	18.8	18.2	20.4
18:3	5.4	5.5	6.4	7.2	5.8	6.3
20:4	0.3	0.0	<0.1	0.5	0.3	0.3
			Free fatty acids			
16:0	30.6	34.0	27.1	30.2	36.5	31.9
16:1	4.4	4.9	4.7	3.8	3.5	2.8
18:0	7.5	8.3	5.9	9.4	11.8	8.3
18:1	20.6	21.5	16.5	19.8	18.8	18.1
18:2	19.8	17.4	20.0	14.1	11.5	19.4
18:3	8.3	9.0	14.1	9.4	5.9	8.3
20:4	0.4	0.7	2.4	1.9	1.2	1.4
			Phospholipids			
16:0	19.4	20.5	25.9	22.8	24.2	24.7
16:1	1.6	1.3	1.0	0.9	0.9	1.0
18:0	22.6	25.9	20.3	20.5	22.4	20.7
18:1	11.3	9.2	13.8	14.6	11.4	12.2
18:2	29.8	29.7	27.6	28.5	28.5	29.0
18:3	4.5	2.5	2.4	2.8	2.7	3.0
20:4	3.6	6.3	4.8	5.0	6.3	5.6

Fatty acids are designated by chain length:no. of double bonds. Percentages were determined by gas–liquid chromatography. SEM values were obtained for all mean values shown, but since they were all closely similar to those in columns 1 and 2, they are not displayed.

* Group C. Number of animals (n) = 7.

† Group A (thoracic, n = 6) and Group B (hepatic, n = 5)

to deposit these data with the American Society for Information Science and not clutter up his table by including them.

Finally, how many statistical data should be given in such an instance? Those shown in Table 7 represent the absolute minimum; other authors might be inclined to add standard errors for all mean values. But if the author points out that all percentages were obtained by the same technique, those given in Table 7 are enough to show that the differences between the first two data columns are going to be highly significant, while those between the other columns are not—which is the whole point of the table. Thus the completeness I advocated in the above section on *Statistics* must, like all principles in writing, be subjected to considerations of common sense, one of the most valuable attributes you can possibly develop in your students.

FIGURES

Figures fall into two distinct categories: those in which numerical data have been transformed into graphs, and those which actually present primary evidence of the scientific observations reported. The second category includes instrumental tracings (e.g., the various kinds of spectra); photographs of (for example) organisms, thin-layer chromatographic plates, or paper electrophoresis strips; and light- or electron micrographs. Your discipline may require still other types, such as maps and charts. Distinguish between the categories, but point out that all figures have two things in common: they all have legends, written by the author, and they all have a shape, determined by the author.

Legends, so often hurriedly tacked onto the manuscript at the very end, form a vital part of the figure and can be a potent force in the article. They consist of a *title*, which orients the reader toward the interpretation and meaning of the figure, followed by an *explanation* of symbols and images within the figure so that it can be intelligently examined, and in many instances *experimental details* about how the figure was obtained. Thus, the figure, with its legend, is a complete unit of communication, just as a table with its accompanying material is.

On the subject of the shape of figures, point out that the shape of graphs can be determined almost arbitrarily by appropriate choice of scale. Hence, as soon as the student begins to design his graphs he should consider the format of the journal he has selected and how the graphs can best be fitted into one or more of its columns. Photographs of instruments or objects may not be so elastic, but often a thoughtful selection of the critical portion of the field of view will prevent disastrous reduction of the whole when the article is printed.

Now go on to consider each type of figure separately. If you want more material than is given below, see the *CBE Style Manual*, pp. 67–80 of the 5th edition.

Graphs

Purpose

When he is planning his graphs, as in all steps in the preparation of a manuscript, the writer must be acutely aware of the *purpose* of what he is doing. In general, the graphing of data that could otherwise appear in a table is justified only when the more vivid display of those data leads to a faster comparison of relationships between them. Thus the purpose of graphs is to promote understanding of the results and to suggest interpretations of their meaning.

Form

Several possible forms exist, but the most useful ones in scientific work are the plotted curve and the histogram. The data points on which the curve is based must, of course, be shown; refer your students to standard texts (e.g., *CBE Style Manual*, p. 69 of 5th ed.) for the preferred symbols. Stress the important principle that one must never extrapolate a line or curve outside the points observed without making the reader fully aware of the extrapolation and its inherent dangers. This should lead the student to consider whether it is even appropriate to draw a curve *between* the observed values or whether the histogram representation, with no continuum implied, is the more appropriate form to use. Considerations like this, which stimulate your students to think, are much more valuable to them in the end than detailed discussion of different techniques of graph-making, which will probably be handled by the technical illustrators anyway.

Clarity

Tell your students to spare no effort in making the graph as clear as possible. Although published graphs can be more complex than is allowable for slides designed for a talk (see Chapter 13), there is a limit to the number of trends and relationships that can be conveyed by any one graph, and you should train your students to recognize this limitation. Again in the interests of clarity, *axes must be labeled*—intelligibly yet compactly, and complete with the units of measure. A little thought will give the units that will require the least number of digits along the axes. Finally, all extraneous background material must be eliminated. For practical help on the technical side, refer your students to the two books cited under "Graphs" at the beginning of this chaper (p. 115).

Truth

Although a pleasing appearance in a graph is a worthy aim, emphasize that students must never sacrifice scientific truth to esthetic appeal. Reiterate the point about unjustified extrapolation. Illustrate the possibility that a choice of scale to achieve a certain over-all shape may falsify the impression of the results. Encourage all students to show not merely mean values but vertical bars for SD or SEM in their graphs, and to make clear in the legend whether SD or SEM is represented and what is the value of *n*. See whether they can devise some graphical method of distinguishing between a series of values obtained for a single experimental animal subjected to several samplings after treatment and values from different animals sampled independently. There is no standard method for doing this, but thinking about the problem may develop their ability to devise principles of graph-making for themselves.

Instrumental Tracings

Is it essential for the reader that he actually see the trace provided by an automatically actuated pen on a recording chart? How necessary is it to present the UV, IR, or NMR spectrum, the densitometric tracing or the fluctuating concentration of a chromatographic effluent? These are the questions that the author must ask before he plans to present such tracings as figures. Too often, it seems, an author rather thoughtlessly decides to include this kind of evidence, merely because it is something tangible, when a line or two of text would give exactly the same information far more economically.

Get your students into the habit, therefore, of asking these questions, and elicit from them some general principles about the answers they are likely to give. UV spectra, for example, are rarely complex enough to justify reproduction. The same goes for any curve consisting of a single peak of unremarkable shape or several widely spread peaks whose relative height and position can be unequivocally specified in writing. When IR or NMR spectra are used merely to identify a compound by comparison with published spectra, and the curves are indeed identical, the new one need not be published. After all, the reader accepts the author's word on a melting point or optical rotation, observation of which cannot be reproduced in the pages of a journal—so why should he expect proof of a simple statement about the spectrum, just because the technique affords a visual trace?

An instrumental tracing should be shown, however, if

(a) it relates to a new compound;
(b) it is open to several interpretations;
(c) several parts of it remain unexplained or unidentified;
(d) the article describes an instrument or technique of which the tracing is the product;
(e) the shapes of peaks are to be analyzed mathematically or compared with a theoretical shape.

Clearly, the decision about any particular tracing has to be made on its own merits, but you will find that your students are capable of making such decisions quite well, without detailed guidance. Once they learn to ask "Is this tracing really necessary?" common sense will do the rest.

Half-tones

The same questions should arise here as for instrumental tracings: will a figure based on this photograph add something vital to the information offered? In addition, however, the author must be aware that clarity comparable with that in a tracing can be achieved for a half-tone only at considerably increased trouble and expense. Schlieren traces are a case in point. They are often reproduced as evidence of purity (assessed by ultracentrifugation) when a statement would suffice; very gloomy they look, and furthermore often undecipherable, except in broad outline.

On the other hand, a photograph of a thin-layer chromatographic plate or a paper electrophoresis strip often does provide more information than a statement about *RF* values or relative mobilities of the major components, and the information is of a kind difficult to put succinctly into words: the shape of spots, degree of overlap, etc. Although publication of such half-tones can therefore be valuable, the writer should not regard it as obligatory.

When new apparatus is being described, photographs of it are often provided. Here, train your students to ask themselves whether a diagram would not actually be more illuminating. If the half-tone really has some advantage over a drawing (which is rare), advise them always to consult a technical illustrator before taking the photograph or arranging for it to be taken.

Micrographs

Most students know—because of their delight in esoteric knowledge—that electron micrographs are difficult to reproduce in a journal with all the exquisite refinement of detail of which the electron microscope is capable. If they are engaged in this kind of work, they will have chosen a journal with proved capabilities in fine engraving and printing. Photographs taken through a light microscope are less critical, but should also be examined for high quality, because, in the course of the whole printing process, the image is transferred several times from one surface to another and loses a little sharpness at each transfer.

Once the photographs have been chosen for quality and for the message they are intended to convey, the author must look at each one separately, from the reader's point of view. He should give the reader as much help as possible, for example by selecting the center of the field to coincide with the center of interest, by cropping the print to a shape suitable for the journal without reduction in size, and by affixing arrows and letters to identify portions of the field and to direct attention to the features of interest. Inclusion of a bar to represent 10 μm, 10 nm, or any length appropriate to the scale, in a corner of the photograph rapidly orients the reader even though, when the magnification is given in the legend, it is not strictly necessary.

In addition to the general precepts about legends that you have already given, add here the items that an author must remember to include in legends to micrographs: the type of stain, or other essential treatment used to obtain the image; the identification of every letter attached to the photograph; and the degree of magnification.

CONCLUSION

This chapter has dealt with principles and not with graphic techniques, since in research work—whether it is carried out in university, government department, or industry—the scientist usually has access to technical illustrators with greater experience than he can ever hope to acquire, and he should learn to avail himself of this expert knowledge. But only he, as author, can accurately visualize his readers and foresee the scope and limits of his article. Only he, therefore, can gauge whether to use tables or figures and, if so, which and how many of them; only he can make the multitudinous decisions that lead to well-designed illustrative material. For these decisions he needs training in understanding the *purposes* and *principles* of illustrations. Don't bore your students teaching them how to draw and letter; teach them, rather, how to think.

11

Preparation for Writing the Doctoral Thesis

YOU SHOULD READ IF POSSIBLE:

Pages 1–31 in:
Almack, John C. *Research and Thesis Writing*. 1930. Houghton Mifflin, Boston (out of print)

Page 1–64 in:
Freedman, Paul. *The Principles of Scientific Research*. 1960. Pergamon Press, Oxford and New York, 2nd ed. (out of print)

Pages 1–17 in:
McCartney, Eugene S. *Recurrent Maladies in Scholarly Writing*. 1969. Gordian Press, Staten Island, NY (reprint of 1953 ed.)

Pages 1–18 in:
Peterson, Martin S. *Scientific Thinking and Scientific Writing*. 1961. Reinhold, New York (out of print)

When he is preparing to write his doctoral thesis, a graduate student looks, of course, to his own research supervisor for guidance. You, the instructor in scientific writing, may wonder what business you have interfering with this arrangement. It is true that the ultimate responsibility for preparing the student to write his thesis rests with each supervisor. However, you can provide your colleagues with an invaluable starting point in discharging this responsibility if you add to your instruction on writing a journal article some class discussions on writing a thesis. "Is there, in fact, any essential difference between the two writing tasks?" should, I think, be the central question to which these discussions are addressed.

In my opinion, the principles to be applied to writing a thesis are identical with those to be applied to writing a journal article. Both forms call for the same self-discipline, the same hard thinking, and clear, logical, concise writing. Yet, because theses are not subject to the limitations of space imposed by editors of professional journals, the notion has unfortunately got about that the style of writing in scientific theses should be quite different from that in journal articles. The freedom from spatial restriction is too often taken as permission to include every unimportant detail and to prose along in intolerably verbose passages; and the nervous candidate, looking over the efforts of his predecessors, feels obliged to be just as tedious as they were for fear his slim volume will seem trivial by comparison.

Theses do not have to be thick to be scholarly. Most true scholars, remembering the long hours of work needed to attain precision and conciseness, would tend, on the contrary, to give the palm for diligence to writers who are brief—if any such could be found. A single major journal article, in which a great deal of work is represented in condensed form, would in many cases be a better measure of a candidate's performance than the usual kind of dissertation now being accepted. However, it is unlikely that more than a few graduate schools will unshackle themselves from tradition to the extent of accepting published articles in lieu of a dissertation (although this is the practice in Sweden, where the doctorate is by no means less demanding than here). Let us therefore consider how we can retain the dissertation's traditional form but regard it, more rationally, as a piece of scientific writing in which the author must meet the same high standards as in later professional publications.

A convenient classroom approach to this subject is for you to solicit and list on the blackboard characteristics of a journal article and of a doctoral dissertation, as though you intend to define some essential differences between the two forms of writing. A few of the distinguishing characteristics generally ascribed to a thesis are listed in Table 1. After several entries have been tabulated ask the question "Which of these supposed differences are both necessary and useful if the purposes of a thesis are to be fulfilled?" A group discussion of such a list will usually confirm that a thesis differs from a journal article in only a few ways, namely those designated A to C in Table 1. Some notes on these features follow.

A *The thesis is an educational tool.* Educators (and students) often make the mistake of regarding the thesis as a measure of the student's *activity* during the educational period instead of as a measure of his *preparedness* for the professional life that follows. The student therefore tends to describe a multitude of details (like a doctoral student) instead of trying

TABLE 1 *Characteristics of a Thesis (as distinguished from a journal article)*

A thesis:

A	is an educational tool
B	is the result of individual, not team, research
C	may present more than one topic
D	presents a formal statement of hypothesis
E	contains a detailed review of the literature
F	presents all the data obtained in the study
G	offers an extended and argumentative discussion
H	summarizes the results and conclusions
J	lists a comprehensive bibliography

to make his thesis a coherent, concise unit of scientific communication (like a mature scientist). To me this seems contrary to the educational purpose.

B *The thesis is the result of individual research.* This distinguishing feature means that the thesis will bear only one author's name. Since a dissertation represents the student's first individual investigation, it should demonstrate his ability to define a problem, to choose appropriate methods for solving the problem, and to present his results and conclusions clearly and fairly. Convincing demonstration of such ability will result only if the student exercises a strong sense of relevance and functional economy, as we have advocated in the writing of a journal article.

C *The thesis may cover several different approaches to a problem.* Each of these may best be presented as a separate chapter, and in this regard the thesis may resemble a book rather than a journal article. Greater control over consistency is therefore needed, as well as an even more detailed outline to help the student maintain an over-all grasp of the dissertation as it takes shape.

Careful examination of the remaining "distinguishing features" shows that the distinctions they purport to convey are false ones. If (D) a journal article does *not* present a formal hypothesis, it is deficient: many articles fail to communicate, precisely because the hypothesis on which the work is based is not enunciated. Although (E) the dissertation traditionally contains an exhaustive review of the literature, you should make it clear that it is not the place for extensive, uncritical listing of others' results. In a similar manner, the dissertation has traditionally become (F) a repository of all data, often only marginally relevant, that the student has collected. Sometimes, these data might be regarded as potentially useful in the future, and if the student is convinced of this he can allow himself to put them in an appendix—but not in the body of the thesis, which should present results as succinctly as in a journal. An extensive and argumentative discussion (G) may occasionally be allowable in a dissertation, but only within reasonable limits (see below), which are scarcely broader than for an article. The results and conclusions *must* be summarized (H), but this is true of journal articles too; and a comprehensive bibliography (J) is usually much inferior to a selective one if the student wants to demonstrate his scientific discrimination and ability.

Try to guide discussion of these matters in such a way that the students themselves conclude that a concise, closely-reasoned dissertation is better than a bulky one. They will be interested in a description, along the following lines, of the history of the thesis as an educational tool. After that, Webster's excellent definition of a scholar will lead you very neatly into a discussion of the most desirable characteristics of the various sections that scholarly dissertations commonly contain.

What Is a Thesis?

Historically, the thesis has changed considerably—from an oral defense of a proposition by the student against all comers in the university to a written description of research that leads to a hypothesis put forward by the student (1). Skill in the logical written presentation of ideas has replaced skill in disputation as the criterion for judging a student's accomplishment. A demonstrated ability to do independent research has been added to the old requirement that the student master the basic principles of knowledge in a particular field of endeavor. The doctoral thesis, therefore, represents the culmination of several years of intensive effort of education and research, and is an exhibit of the mental prowess of the student.

At this point, you can discuss the several manuals that are available on thesis writing (refs. 2–4), but you should point out that they are primarily concerned with details of format and mechanics of construction. Our concern is more with the mental preparation of the student before the task of writing begins than with the details of writing. Most of the principles of writing dealt with in Chapters 1–8 and 10 of this manual are applicable to the thesis, and will not be repeated here.

You should also introduce the student to the literature available on the philosophy of science (5, 6) and the art of scientific investigation (7). This is a large subject, but it would be useful to the student to review and discuss some of the values of logic, intuition, explanation, and proof in conducting research, and to think about the applications of these concepts of philosophy to a thesis. Such a discussion admittedly expands the scope of the subject to include methods of research, but this is a concrete way of emphasizing that the student must produce a "scholarly dissertation."

What Is Meant by a Scholarly Dissertation?

Webster's Third New International Dictionary gives two contrasting definitions of a scholar. The first is "one who attends a school or studies under a teacher." The second is "one who by long systematic study (as in a university) has gained a high degree of mastery in one or more of the academic disciplines; esp. one who has engaged in advanced study and acquired the minutiae of knowledge in some special field along with accuracy and skill in investigation and powers of critical analysis in interpretation of such knowledge." The second definition is more to our purpose in describing the level of intellectual achievement necessary for the Doctor of Philosophy.

Certain words and phrases stand out as important attributes in Webster's definition, e.g., "high degree of mastery," "accuracy and skill in investigation," and "critical analysis in interpretation," and these can be singled out as the keys to a successful thesis. You should take the time to emphasize that these are characteristics *of the student* and are painstakingly acquired long before the thesis is attempted. These attributes will be seen between the lines of the thesis despite attempts to hide shortcomings by flowery prose, long quotations, and an extensive bibliography. Unless the thesis clearly demonstrates that the student has mastered the subject, is a skilled investigator, and has a critical mind, the thesis can scarcely be judged "a scholarly dissertation."

At this point, you should briefly describe an accepted general format for a doctoral thesis—for example, introduction, methods, results, and discussion. Such a description will be useful in presenting the following ideas concerning scholarship and will offer the student a framework of reference for questions or comments.

How Does One Indicate a "High Degree of Mastery" of a Subject?

The *Introduction* of a thesis is the first item to be read, and its content and presentation will largely determine, in the reader's mind, whether the entire thesis is worth perusing. Many instructions for preparing theses favor separating both a statement of the problem and a review of the literature from the general introduction. This makes neat small paragraphs with tidy subheadings, but is a less effective way of indicating competence in a subject area than a complete integration of these items in one concise answer to two questions: "What is the problem under investigation?" and "Why did you select this one for study?" Here the student has a chance to pick and choose from the assembled mass of good and bad published reports and to construct a rational statement of the problem.

You have an opportunity here to introduce the role of intuition and speculation in developing a working hypothesis. To be acceptable, however, such a hypothesis must be testable, and the student is obliged to present a reasonable plan for such a test. Speculation without testing is to be discouraged; this cardinal principle of science was laid down by William Occam—"theoretical existences are not to be increased without necessity."

Nowadays a complete review of the literature is a physical impossibility for most theses. Any attempt to do this by presenting conflicting sides of all pertinent questions in great detail is not only unsatisfactory; it is strong evidence that the student has learned to read and write, but cannot think. If the student shirks his responsibility for making judgments of the value of published reports in relation to his study, how can he hope to convince the reading committee that he has mastered his subject? At the end of a thorough search of the literature, the student should be better qualified to make these decisions than anyone else. A historical record of all false leads and all mistakes in investigation may make interesting reading to some, but in a thesis such a record sows seeds of doubt as to the competence and self-reliance of the student.

I see no real need for a separate answer to the question "Why did you select this problem for study?" A clear, concise statement of the problem will usually indicate that the study under investigation is part of a more general one that bears a direct relation to a basic principle of science or a pressing human need. If the reader at this point still is asking "Why?" the chances are that the introduction needs some rethinking and then rewriting.

How Does One Indicate "Accuracy and Skill in Investigation"?

All theses should have a section dealing with *Methods and Materials* and the accuracy inherent in the methods. In this section all the excuses are made for errors of omission, faulty techniques, and lack of sufficient data for making meaningful comparisons. It is presumed that a good thesis will have a minimum of these excuses, but some show of humility and an awareness of the fallibility of human endeavor will not be construed by an intelligent reader as a significant weakness.

The student may be excused for a rather lengthy description of methodology, unless the methods are standard and readily available to the reader. If a lengthy description is planned, however, the student must train himself to be considerate of the reader and provide an over-all sketch of how the study was done, so the reader may be sustained through the arid passages or enabled to skip them without serious loss.

The student should be cautioned against being overly critical of the methods finally selected for use. Full analysis and criticism of the methods should be made before the study is attempted. If no rational or possible approach to a study presents itself, the wisest course is to look for another problem. No worse criticism of the skill of an investigator can be heard than "He is a hard worker, but the problem he chose was impossible." Once a problem has been selected, and a reasonable approach has been decided upon, the student should look on the bright side and indicate what can be accomplished with the methods.

The meat of the thesis is found in a section usually indicated as *Results*. Impress upon the student that only the results of *his* investigation are to be put here. Presentation of a mixture of the student's data and other published work leads to utter confusion. It also betrays a lack of confidence: the student seems unsure that he can draw reliable conclusions from his results. A skilled investigator knows beforehand what others have found, has analyzed the omissions and faulty techniques, and has designed his procedures to correct these faults. When the main points of the results are logically presented in the text and corroborated by factual data in tables and figures, there should be no need to beg for confirmation by citing another investigator who found the same or a similar thing to be true.

How Does One Indicate "Critical Analysis in Interpretation"?

When a student comes to the point of discussing his study in relation to previous and future work, he stands naked before his professional mentors. Here is the place where his philosophy, his relationship to his colleagues, his scientific attitude, yes, even his religion, come to the forefront. Here is where the great gamble is taken, if he so desires. A discussion can be very brief and conservative, limited to a few unequivocal statements, and ending with a statement that more needs to be done. Or it can be an ingenious and imaginative discourse on what the study may mean in relation to a major problem in the field. The student here can be granted considerable license in speculative thought, provided he pays due regard to rules of logic and inference, and takes care to remain relevant to his topic. He will not be judged harshly if he chooses the popular, conservative course of action. But neither is he likely to be considered a "thoughtful observer of the contemporary scene" unless he attempts to put his work into the perspective of the present state of knowledge.

What Is a Thesis?

To sum up, a thesis may be likened to the reflection of a portion of the student's mind. It should be a rational discourse on a problem in science. Success in presenting a thesis of words, phrases, and paragraphs will depend to a great extent on the preparation of the mind that conceives it. Training in scientific procedures and philosophy, in reading and writing, and above all in disciplined thinking, thus become an integral part of the image conveyed to the reader.

If I were asked for a single measure of scholarship, a single indicator of disciplined thinking, and therefore the best single criterion of a good thesis, I would put forward a plea for simplicity. This quality is, unfortunately, the one most conspicuously lacking in present-day theses and the one least prized among ambitious young scientists.

"Simplicity, paradoxically, is the outward sign and symbol of depth of thought. It seems to me simplicity is about the most difficult thing to achieve in scholarship and writing. How difficult is clarity of thought, and yet it is only as thought becomes clear that simplicity is possible. When we see a writer belaboring an idea we may be sure that the idea is belaboring him."(8)

References

1. Almack, John C. *Research and Thesis Writing*. 1930. Houghton Mifflin, Boston.
2. McCartney, E. S. *Recurrent Maladies in Scholarly Writing*. 1969. Gordian Press, Staten Island, NY.
3. Campbell, W. G. et al. *Form and Style: Theses, Reports, Term Papers*. 6th ed. 1981. Houghton Mifflin, Boston.
4. Turabian, K. L. *A Manual for Writers of Term Papers, Theses and Dissertations*. 4th ed. 1973. University of Chicago Press, Chicago.
5. Popper, K. *The Logic of Scientific Discovery*. 1976. Harper and Row, New York; Hutchinson, London.
6. Shapere, Dudley. *Philosophical Problems of Natural Science*. 1965. The Macmillan Co., New York and London.
7. Beveridge, W. I. B. *The Art of Scientific Investigation*. 1960. Random House, New York; Heinemann, London.
8. Lin Yutang. *The Importance of Living*. 1937. John Day, Reynal and Hitchcock, New York; Heinemann, London (1938). p. 81.

Further Reading

Harman, E. and Montagnes, I. (ed.) *The Thesis and the Book*. 1976. University of Toronto Press, Toronto.

Recommendations for Presentation of Theses. BS 4821: 1972. British Standards Institution, London.

12

Writing a Research Project Proposal

YOU SHOULD READ:

White, V. *Grants: How to Find Out About Them and What To Do Next.* 1975. Plenum Press, New York.

White, V. *Grant Proposals That Succeeded.* 1983. Plenum Press, New York and London.

Several authors. The project grant application to the National Institutes of Health. *Fed. Proc.* 1973; 32: 1541–1550.

YOU WILL NEED:

The instructions and application forms for grants from any large government agency.

Like other kinds of scientific writing, the writing of a project proposal demands considerable judgment. If the judgment is to be good, the writer must learn all he can about those who will read the proposal, and keep those readers constantly in mind as he writes. You may feel that your students are at too early a stage in their careers to be interested in learning how to write project proposals, and it is true that their first journal article will probably be more imminent than their first grant application. But they will enjoy the logic of applying to this easily imagined task the principles of scientific writing given in Chapters 2–8, and if you show them, by using the project proposal as an example, that the steps you have taught them for writing a journal article can be applied to other kinds of writing, you will have done them a great service.

Project proposals differ according to the audience addressed. For example, a description of some proposed research may be submitted to one's immediate superiors directing the research, who may be expected to be familiar with all the details, or to a group of nonscientific directors conscious of, and knowledgeable about, only far-reaching objectives. Or the project proposal may be a grant application submitted more impersonally to a private foundation or to a government agency. Whoever the recipients of a project proposal may be, they will certainly be more concerned with wider aspects of policy than is the writer of the proposal.

For this reason, the writer must be even more concerned with *summarizing* features than when he is writing a journal article. Thus, he should give still more attention to his title and his abstract, which should be not only concisely descriptive and clearly purposeful, but provocative and stimulating as well. After all, he hopes to interest his readers in the proposal, and convince them it is worthwhile. He should plan to include a Contents page, both for easy reference and to give the reader a bird's-eye view of the proposal right at the start. A clear Statement of Purpose should be an early feature and a statement of Expected Results a late one—both listed in the Contents page. And it is not too much to add an Outline of long or complex passages at the point where they begin. By the same token, the main contours of the budget can usefully appear long before the detailed breakdown of projected costs.

Having enunciated these general principles, go through Steps 1–25 of Writing a Journal Article and show how, with very little change to suit the circumstances, these steps can be used for guidance in writing a project proposal.

STEP 1: *What Is the Right Time to Prepare a Proposal?*

Unlike the answer to "What is the Right Time to Publish?" which is often "Later than your inclinations suggest," the answer to this question is "Sooner than you think." Grant applications usually take *at least* six months to be acted on, and a well-prepared application can take two months to be put together. Twelve months, therefore, seems a minimum to allow before the date on which the work is to begin.

STEP 2: *What Question Will Be Asked, and What Answers Are Expected?*

Teach your students to put the answers to these queries in writing, in preparation for the all-important Statements of Purpose and of Expected Results.

STEP 3: *What Is the Most Suitable Agency?*

Although in writing a project proposal the author is concerned not with publication but with highly restricted circulation of his document, the question of audience is still of paramount importance. Disabuse your students' minds of the notion that foundations and government agencies are mere offices for the automatic distribution of unlimited funds to those who apply for them; on the contrary, all are guided by policies and purposes that the applicant should study closely before he decides where his best chances of success lie.

The Catalog of Federal Domestic Assistance (1) describes the purpose and scope of U.S. federal granting agencies, but your students will have to work harder to obtain corresponding information from other grant-giving bodies. They might consult the latest annual report or other statement of the agency's activities, the list of research projects currently supported, or any of the agency's other publications. Get the students to find out, using a selected list of foundations, what can be discovered by direct inquiry about the scope of a foundation's activity.

STEP 4: *How Is the Project Related to the Existing Body of Knowledge?*

It is essential that the applicant make a good showing when he describes the published investigations leading to the one he now proposes. His search of the literature must be thorough and thoughtful, or woe betide him when the application is reviewed. He must demonstrate both irrefutable logic and imaginative insight if he is to persuade hardheaded scientists that a gap remains to be filled or that extensions of established lines of research promise rich scientific rewards. Make clear to your students that the case for the project will have to be tightly argued in the proposal itself; in Step 4 the author prepares himself for this close reasoning by writing down succinctly the basic premises from which he will work and seeing whether they lead convincingly to the plan that he will formulate.

STEP 5: *Write the Title and Synopsis*

This first statement of what the proposal will cover and, by implication, what it will leave out, serves the same purpose of drawing up the ground plan as in the journal article. Title and synopsis derive directly from Step 2. The synopsis will be reworked later into the General Project Description that all application forms overtly or implicitly require.

STEP 6: *Match Title and Synopsis to the Purpose and Scope of the Chosen Agency*

Your students will by now recognize the value of comparing the definite written form of their proposal (Step 5) with the avowed or patent objectives of the group they hope will support it. From here on the aims and desires of that group should be constantly present in the applicant's mind.

STEP 7: *Read the Instructions to Applicants*

Some agencies supply printed application forms with detailed and complete instructions on how they are to be filled out. You should get some of these for your students to study. Agencies that provide no forms frequently base their judgment of the merit of an application, and of the ability of the applicant to conduct the research, on the skill with which the application is organized. If instructions do exist, they should be carefully studied at this stage, since adherence to them may make all the difference between failure and success.

STEP 8: *Decide on the Basic Form of the Proposal*

Again, if application forms are provided, the basic form of the proposal is automatically determined, and the applicant is left to exercise his judgment only in the matter of degree of detail in the various sections. Otherwise, a good basic scheme is: brief introduction, concluding with the statement of purpose; general description of proposal; methods; expected results; and discussion, primarily of the significance of the proposed work with respect to the objectives of the agency applied to. The basic scheme is not grossly different from that of a journal article up to this point. To it must be added evidence of the applicant's ability to carry out the work (his position, previous publications, honors and awards) and the facilities available to him—and, of course, estimates of what the project will cost, with justification where necessary.

STEP 9: *Stock the Section Reservoirs*

Here you can advocate exactly the same method as for writing a journal article.

STEP 10: *Construct Tables and Figures*

Tables and figures should be used with the same purpose as in a journal article: to convey information succinctly and vividly. The data underlying the illustrations may be from others or from preliminary experiments.

STEPS 11 and 12: *Construct the Topic and Sentence Outlines*

Because continuity of thought and a logical sequence of ideas are likely to move the readers to favorable action, sound outlines may be even more important in a project proposal than in a journal article. For the same reason urge your students to follow *Step 13*: "Write the first draft of the proposal continuously from beginning to end."

STEP 14: *Introduction and General Description of Project*

For the same reasons given in Chapter 4, the description of work preceding the proposed research should be selective rather than exhaustive, and confined to significant references. The introduction must lead clearly to the project description.

STEP 15: *Construct the List of References As You Go Along*

In most applications it is usual to give references within the text rather than in a separate bibliography, so that the need to check bibliographic details becomes evident during the writing. Once again, urge your students to acquire the habit of checking references early.

STEPS 16-18: *Methods, Expected Results, and Discussion Sections*

Most of the principles needed in these sections have already been touched on. Remind your students to think clearly about the purpose of the document: for example, in the Methods section the object is not, as in a journal article, to enable a trained investigator who reads the proposal to do the work, but to demonstrate that the applicant is familiar with the methods available and chooses from them wisely. In Expected Results, exaggerated predictions should be avoided; nevertheless, the widest potential significance of the work must be brought out in the Discussion.

STEPS 19-25

The remaining steps in writing a journal article (see Chapters 5–8) apply almost without change to writing a project proposal. Remind your students what the steps are, and point out that the technique they have learned for one type of scientific writing will stand them in good stead in many others. Impress on them that in the less "scientific" parts of the proposal, those that deal not with the project but with the applicant, they should not allow a feeling of false modesty to lead them into affected circumlocutions, but should maintain the same clean scientific style—brief, simple, and direct—throughout the proposal. Deviousness of any kind is to be avoided, and the applicant's best chance of success, here as in all kinds of scientific writing, lies in honesty and clarity of purpose.

* * *

Writing a project proposal is a considerable undertaking. You may decide to give it instead of a journal article as the major assignment of the writing course, as suggested in Chapter 2, or you may make it an additional assignment if time permits. In either case, I suggest that the proposal be written as though for a large governmental agency that does *not* have a prescribed outline, so that the students experience maximum challenge in organizing this piece of writing.

Help your students to visualize the audience they are writing for by listing the criteria by which the worth of every application for financial support is judged:

Validity of the central concept

Soundness of experimental design and appropriateness of methods selected

Significance in terms both of pure science and of regional or national priorities

Relevance to the over-all program of the funding agency

Competence of the personnel who are to conduct the research

Adequacy of the research facilities

Appropriateness of the budget (too modest a budget can be as damaging as an overblown one in indicating the applicant's poor judgment).

Reference

1. Executive Office of the President, Office of Management and Budget. *Catalog of Federal Domestic Assistance*. Published annually (Washington, DC).

Further Reading

DeBakey, L. The persuasive proposal. *J. Tech. Writing and Communication*. 1976; 6:5–25.

DeBakey, L. and DeBakey, S. The art of persuasion: logic and language in proposal writing. *Grants Magazine* 1978; 1:43–60.

Eaves, G.N. Who reads your project-grant applications to the National Institutes of Health? *Fed. Proc*. 1972; 31:2–9.

Merritt, D.H. Grantsmanship: an exercise in lucid presentation. *Clin. Res*. 1963; 11:375–377.

13

Oral Presentation of a Scientific Paper

EDITOR'S PREFACE:

Some justification may seem necessary for including a chapter about speaking in a book about writing. We do not intend, however, to be apologetic about this inclusion because no one will dispute that formal talks at local, national, or international meetings are often closely linked—as elements in the transmission of knowledge—with publication of the same work in an archival journal. From an organizational point of view, planning an article and planning a talk are identical up to a certain point, while the same principles of scientific style apply throughout. Didactically, the juxtaposition of a course on writing with a subsequent short course on oral presentation is excellent for teaching the similarities and differences between the two modes of communication. Finally, the writing that is necessary in the early stages of planning a talk provides yet another concrete example for your students of the postulate (see Chapter 2) that writing clarifies thought.

TIMING:

Three to four one-hour sessions are sufficient. Principles can be dealt with, and exemplified by a 10-minute talk of your own, in the first two hours; in each subsequent hour three ten-minute talks can be given by the students and critically discussed, as explained in the chapter. These "rehearsal" sessions can be continued as long as you think them useful to the nonperformers (they are always useful to the performers).

YOU WILL PROBABLY FIND THE FOLLOWING MATERIAL USEFUL:

American National Standards Institute. *Preparation of Scientific Papers for Written or Oral Presentation*. ANSI, New York. Z39.16-1972

Booth, V. *Communication in Science: Writing and Speaking*. 1984. Cambridge University Press, Cambridge and New York.

Casey, Robert S. *Oral Communication of Technical Information*. 1958. Reinhold, New York and London.

Hays, Robert. Including visual aids in reports. Chapter 10 of *Principles of Technical Writing*. 1965. Addison-Wesley, Reading, MA.

Jones, B. A. The oral report, its preparation and presentation. Chapter 7 of *The Technical Report* (Benjamin H. Weil, editor). 1954. Reinhold, New York and London.

Norgaard, M. The text of a speech. Chapter 11, Section XV of *Technical Writer's Handbook*. 1959. Harper and Bros., New York.

Weiss, H., and J. B. McGrath, Jr. *Technically Speaking*. 1963. McGraw-Hill, New York and London.

Woodford, F. P. Improving the communication of scientific information. *BioScience* 1969; 19:625–627.

Oral communication plays an important part in the exchange of scientific information. The main purpose of a congress—oral discussion between participants—can be achieved only if a contribution is heard and understood. Scientists often travel thousands of miles to a congress, and each participant should feel duty-bound to be informative, interesting, and concise.

A delivered paper can have a dismal reception for many reasons, but often the main one is that because the proceedings of the conference are to be published, the speaker mistakenly regards his talk as a form of publication. He prepares the talk carefully, and dutifully reads it word for word from his manuscript. Students may be very ready to accept your statement that this is not recommended, but it is well worth the time to discuss with them why it is a bad practice. Point out the differences between oral and written communication—the finite attention span of a listener, the frequent presence of distractions in the auditorium, the inability of a listener to go back over a difficult sentence or to request that an inaudible one be repeated—and show how these considerations should induce the potential speaker to:

1. Capture the full attention of the audience at the very beginning.
2. State the underlying objectives of the research with even greater clarity and emphasis than in written articles.
3. Concentrate on concepts, and eliminate confusing details.
4. Discuss the purpose of each experiment, the conclusions drawn from it, and its connection with the main argument at the time that the results are shown, rather than in a separate "Discussion" section.

5. Present important ideas in several different ways, even at the risk of repetition (an undesirable trait in written presentation).
6. Use slides of lesser complexity than published figures and tables.

This chapter suggests some of the ground rules for an effective oral presentation. Most of what follows is applicable to a 10- or 15-minute presentation, since such short periods are frequently allotted for papers at large-scale scientific meetings. If a student can master the 10-minute talk, he should have little trouble—except, perhaps, that of providing variety of pace and pitch—with longer talks, for the difficulty most people experience consists not in finding enough to say but in condensing what they have to say into the time allowed.

Organization

Should one write out the talk? Yes, but never read it (the reasons will be discussed later). Once the talk is organized through writing, the text can be reduced to an outline. But it should be written out first, rather than simply outlined, so that one can (a) check the logical development, (b) ensure proper transitions, (c) check sentence length and thereby develop the habit of forming short conversational sentences, (d) search for synonyms for frequently recurring words that would otherwise lead to dullness, (e) discard attractive but inessential items, (f) develop colorful imagery, and (g) ensure that only familiar terms are used.

The shorter the time for an oral presentation, the more difficult is the task of organization. From the beginning, train your students to proportion their time correctly: 10 percent for the introduction, 80 percent for the body of the talk (procedure, results, and conclusions), and 10 percent for the summary.

The Introduction

A speaker often has many things to contend with at the outset. Rooms get overheated and smoky, and the audience may be restive after listening to previous speakers. People may be moving about in the rear of the room, greeting incoming or outgoing friends, rustling the pages of their programs, coughing, and so forth. The opening words of a speech must, therefore, be simple, easily understood, and carefully slanted toward the interests of the audience. One secret of speaking successfully to a large audience is to gain attention with the opening sentences; otherwise it may never be secured at all.

The part of the introduction that precedes the statement of purpose is called the *approach to the audience* because its aim is to arouse interest, to create a friendly and receptive mood, and to prepare the audience to listen and pay attention to the statement of purpose.

Many devices can be employed to capture audience attention, and students should be encouraged to invent examples. Opening with a *narrative* arouses interest because people like to hear stories. ("There is a story of two protein chemists who, encountering each other at the Biochemical Congress in Tokyo, got into an argument about . . . ," or, "One of the most appealing stories in the history of organic chemistry is the one in which Kekulé, jolting along on top of a London bus, suddenly envisioned the benzene molecule in the form of a snake with its tail in its mouth. Unfortunately, the story is inaccurate.")

Opening with a *quotation* is effective if one is chosen that is relevant to the speech and points toward a direct statement of the speaker's purpose. ("Shortly after argon had been discovered, Lord Rayleigh said 'I have seen some indications that the anomalous properties of argon are brought as a kind of accusation against us. But we had the very best intentions in the matter. The facts were too much for us, and all that we can do now is to apologize for ourselves and for the gas. . . .' A somewhat similar situation has arisen with respect to the X-protein, the anomalous properties of which have formed the basis of several unjust accusations. Would it not be preferable to recognize the anomalies, and try to explain them?")

A *rhetorical question* centers attention on the purpose of the study and makes the audience think about the main issue. ("How much do we really know of the mechanism whereby DNA directs the synthesis of RNA?")

Sometimes a *startling statement* will jolt the audience into paying attention. ("Reading our most distinguished scientific journals corrupts the minds of young scientists," or, "Cell membranes seem to be wide open to penetration by all sorts of noxious substances—that is, if you consider them merely as physicochemical barriers.")

A *negative statement* will heighten the "suspense." ("Lowering blood cholesterol levels will not prevent atherosclerosis. At least, there has been no good evidence for this so far.")

A *comparison or contrast* makes a neat opening, particularly if the contrast is a striking one. ("In former times, delicate ladies were carried through the doors of opera houses in sedan chairs to avoid being jostled by the crowd. We are concerned here today with the concept of *carrier molecules* that will transport particular substances safely through the hurly-burly of the cell membrane," or, "Few phenomena are so well understood thermodynamically, or so ill understood kinetically, as the osmotic flow of a solvent through a semipermeable membrane.")

If the speaker knows the *dominant interest* of his audience, he can use it to establish an understanding with them. ("We are all familiar with the thesis that bats use some form of radar to navigate in the darkness. I would like today to offer a novel and unrelated explanation of their skill in avoiding objects under these conditions.")

The attention of a group can usually be caught by listing *specific instances* that relate to a general topic. ("Molecules can pass through a membrane by passive diffusion, or by dissolving in the membrane lipids, or by active transport. Which of these applies to the absorption of bile salts in man?")

Other introductory devices include the practice of starting with a broad statement and *gradually narrowing* it to lead into the purpose of the study being reported; the *descriptive opening* (best suited to papers dealing with new equipment, new techniques, etc.); and the *historical approach.*

Speakers on nontechnical subjects customarily open their talks with a funny story. The pseudohumor of the stock joke ("a funny thing happened to me on the way to the convention hall") is likely to fall flat on its face before an audience of scientists. However, the more subtle humor of asides interpolated throughout the speech is to be encouraged. Still other introductory possibilities include the asking of a question, which the speaker then proceeds to answer immediately; the listing of a series of particulars or a set of vivid details to provide transition to the main thesis; and the use of analogy, where the unknown is paralleled with the known. Examples of several types of openings for a single talk are given in the appendix (pages 165 and 166) to this chapter.

The most obvious device, of course, is to open with a statement of the speaker's purpose. This is certainly one of the most useful when the audience is known to have a direct interest in the topic. However, there are dangers in this straightforward and commonsense approach, which rests on three assumptions: that the listeners have a consuming interest in the topic;

that they have actually heard and understood the title of the talk and studied a previously published abstract; and that they have a thorough knowledge of work on the topic to date. These assumptions may be far from true.

Having (it is to be hoped) captured the interest of the audience, the speaker must state clearly the underlying objectives of the work—why it is of interest—and then give the exact purpose of the experiments to be described. The purpose may be quite a small part of the over-all objectives. There is no shame in this; indeed, the shorter the talk, the more circumscribed the purpose should be. Nothing is more foolish and arrogant than the sickly "Of course I can't really compress four years of work into 15 minutes, but I'll try." The speaker has not been asked to do so, and he has no right to insult his audience by attempting it.

Body of the Talk

Make it clear to your students that the body of a talk requires much the same logical organization of material as an article prepared for publication. The principles of style given in Chapter 6 apply with equal or greater force here. Ideas must be conveyed in short, clear statements (Rule 1). Words must be chosen and used appropriately and precisely (Rule 2) if the listeners are not to be distracted or misled. Vivid language can transform a prosaic talk into a memorable one and speakers should strive to avoid abstract nouns (Rule 3) and to use active rather than passive verbs. The terms used must be readily comprehensible (Rule 4). If the speaker feels that definition of a term is necessary, he must give the definition when the term is first mentioned, taking care not to sound patronizing as he does so.

The purpose of each experiment should be stated and related to the over-all purpose given in the Introduction. This takes time, but the time is well spent because the audience is really in touch with the thread of the argument. Because the time for presentation is limited and the audience is mostly interested in concepts, experimental details must be kept to an absolute minimum. They can always be elicited later during the question-and-answer period when the audience takes the initiative, and, of course, they can be provided in a printed text.

In stating the conclusions from each experiment, the speaker should keep the main purpose of the study in mind and ensure that every point he makes is related to that purpose.

Visual Aids

Visual aids can be effective in maintaining interest, but only if they are used with judgment. They range from a simple tool like the blackboard to complex methods of slide or movie projection. Your students will welcome some discussion of their usefulness and disadvantages.

The use of the blackboard should be confined to small rooms, for people in the back must be able to decipher the message. Blackboard explanations should be planned in advance so that the first part of algebraic symbols or equations or lists will *not* have to be erased to make room for the last parts. Bits of information should not be jotted down in corners of the board, with sweeping lines to indicate where they should have been written in the first place. If circumstances permit, blackboard demonstrations should be *executed* in advance as well, otherwise much valuable time may be lost while the speaker is writing.

Illustrative slides are the most popular form of visual aids, but they, too, pose problems (see Table 1). Remember that slides take time; the audience must be able to understand them fully. At the very least, 1 minute must be allowed for showing and describing a slide, unless it is an extremely simple one shown for a single effect. Demonstrate by example why a graph is preferable to a table and why a simple graph is preferable to one cluttered with more detail than the audience can easily absorb. Let students practice writing captions that are both descriptive and concise and insist that axes be labeled in letters that can be read easily.

Audiences should not be left in the dark throughout the talk, but having the lights constantly flipped on and off can also be distracting. The best compromise is to show well-defined groups of slides, with the lights on between groups. When the speaker wants to provide many data, he will be well advised to show only a small group of slides and supplement them with handouts distributed after the talk (not before, or they, too, will distract the audience's attention!).

The disadvantage of most projection techniques is that while the slide is being projected it replaces the speaker. A notable exception is overhead projection; it complements the speaker because he controls the machine while facing the audience in normal lighting. He can use separate components of a transparency ("vugraphs") to build up a composite image or to disclose information progressively. The versatility of vugraphs in simulating

TABLE 1 *Use of Slides*

Do	Don't
Design	
Allow at least 1 min per slide	Make too many points per slide
Allow time for getting slide on and off	Plan too many slides for time allotted
Allow for accidents to happen	Use tables when graphs are more vivid
Provide titles for slides	Put too many lines on a graph
Plan exactly what to say about each slide	Use unlabeled axes
Technique of making the slide	
Select standard size (2 x 2 or 3¼ x 4 inches)	Use illegibly small numbers
Make material fit a rectangle with long side horizontal	Use square or tall slides unless unavoidable
Use colors if helpful, but not for doubtful esthetic effect	Use white letters on blue or black ground*
Label micrographs to direct audience to point of interest	Use poor-quality prints accompanied by an apology
	Use typewritten slides unless lettered ones are absolutely unavailable†
Presentation	
Ensure slides are in correct order and all the same way up	Keep audience continuously in dark
Locate the pointer before talk	Keep flicking lights off and on
Switch off a flashlight arrow-pointer after each use	Continue to show slide after it is needed
Show slide long enough for comprehension	Read aloud every word on the slide

* Some practitioners maintain stoutly that these "negative" slides are more legible than those with black letters on a white ground. In order not to be dogmatic about it, have your students use the experimental approach and judge for themselves between examples of the same slide made both ways and shown under good and bad conditions in a completely darkened or partly illuminated hall.

† Typewritten slides *can* be legible if all the material that is to be photographed on a 3¼ x 4 inch slide is kept within a rectangle 56 spaces (4.8 inches) wide by 22 spaces (3.7 inches) high, and if a reversed carbon paper is placed behind the paper during the typing. Hand lettering is almost always preferable, however, because the ratio of black lettering to white "blank space" can be increased and because many different sizes of letters can be used.

motion makes them ideal for describing various biological processes.

The professionals in the field of visual aids are the technical illustrators employed by most large institutions. Even if a scientist has mastered the art of graphic presentation in a written article, there is no guarantee that he is also a master at selecting the lettering that will project best. Encourage your students to consult professional illustrators and heed their advice. Too often these artists complain, and with justification, that "every author is an Art Director—he thinks!"

Summary of the Talk

The talk should end with a summary of the ideas presented and leave the audience with the central theme firmly in their minds. Devices for ending the talk include restressing the main points, restating the thesis, concluding with an anecdote, concluding with a question, and concluding by stating a future program.

Outlining the Talk

Once you have impressed upon your students the need for careful preparation and writing of a scientific talk, disabuse their minds of the notion that the talk should be read exactly as written. A speaker cannot hope to hold an audience if he buries his head in a text, raising it only occasionally to reassure himself that he is not alone in the room. Technical material is difficult enough for listeners to absorb without the additional burden of boredom. Train your students, then, to speak either entirely without notes or from a simple outline.

The three most common types are the topic outline, the key-phrase outline, and the sentence outline. The inexperienced speaker is well advised to construct all three in order to fix the organization of the talk in his mind in three different ways. The extent to which a speaker can free himself from the prepared text is usually in direct ratio to his experience as a public speaker. The experienced speaker writes and revises his speech, fixes the main points of the organization in his mind along with some of the key sentences, and uses only a few cards to refresh his memory. On these cards (5 x 7 inches, not smaller) may be written topic headings, key sentences, or transitional sentences; speakers differ on which they find most useful. Suggest to your students that they try all three types. The cards are merely a device to keep the talk in sequence and to avoid the hazards of suddenly going blank. They are the visible end-product of much careful planning, the most important product of which is invisible—a mental image of the intention, structure, and conclusions of the projected talk.

Delivery

Nothing destroys a well-organized talk faster than its delivery in a mumbled monotone by a speaker who obviously wishes he were anywhere except on the platform. Deadly delivery, unintentional punctuation with ah's and er's, and nervous mannerisms evoke an audience reaction ranging from boredom to acute sympathetic embarrassment. All are obstacles that keep the audience from getting the message. Practice and more practice is the solution (more on this in the next section of the chapter).

Speaking Rate, Force, and Pitch

Justly or not, an audience is prone to judge a speaker in great part by the way he sounds. Granting that there is a tremendous range in natural ability, each speaker can, with a little training, make better use of his voice mechanism.

Because good speaking implies that the listeners should be able to think along with the speaker as he talks, a proper speaking rate is essential. It takes practice to avoid talking so quickly that the words are slurred. On the other hand, phrases should not be so dragged out that the audience yearns to supply the words.

The force used in delivery is as important as the rate. In a room that has no provision for mechanical amplification, the best rule is to talk to the people in the back row. Both force and pitch should be varied in a way that emphasizes the main ideas and important parts of the talk, and the longer the talk is to be the more planning should go into this variation. A deadly monotone should be avoided at all costs; the room is probably stuffy enough without giving the audience an additional reason for drifting off to sleep.

Microphone Technique

The increasing availability of mechanical aids permits a speaker to use a more natural voice and still be heard in the back row. However, the mere presence of a microphone does not guarantee that his words will be understood, and amplification emphasizes the speaker's faults as well as any pleasing qualities his voice may have.

Coach your students to stand at least six inches from the microphone; the optimum distance will depend on the strength and quality of a particular voice and on the type of microphone. Have them speak in a natural voice and move away from the instrument slightly when they reach points they wish to emphasize by raising their voices. This will avoid undue amplification. Stress that they must *never* cough or clear their throats directly into the microphone unless they want to sound like the mating call of a bull elephant.

Practice will prevent "mike fright" and ensure that the instrument is a help rather than a hindrance. Once the microphone technique has been acquired, the instrument can be ignored. Be sure your students don't talk directly to it; once they have lost eye contact, they have lost the audience.

Eye Contact

The inexperienced speaker is greatly tempted to look at the floor, the ceiling, out of the window—anywhere, in fact, except at his audience. But eye contact is absolutely essential to effective speaking. One helpful piece of advice is to tell the speaker to pick out several individuals in the audience and speak directly to them in turn—a man near the back row, a lady who looks as though her feet hurt, a man who seems in danger of falling asleep. If he can hold *their* interest, he has it made!

Posture

Posture is a comparatively minor part of delivery, but good posture can contribute much to the impression of relaxation, and the more relaxed the speaker appears to be, the more the audience will be at ease. Warn your students, however, against being excessively informal (hands in pockets, tucked into the belt, etc.), for this can be offensive to a distinguished audience. There is no standardized recommended posture, but there are certain awkward positions that you can help your students avoid. Standing with heels together and toes pointed out at a 45-degree angle tends to make the speaker's legs look tied together. Standing with feet wide apart, as though weathering a gale, will cause a rocking motion that is highly distracting to the audience. A natural stance results when the feet are placed 8 to 10 inches apart, one foot slightly forward of the other. This permits the weight to rest on the foot in back and allows a natural, easy movement when the speaker wants to walk toward the audience or move to right or left. Walking should always be planned and purposeful; aimless wandering about may relax the speaker, but not his listeners.

Gestures

An untrained speaker is extremely self-conscious about gestures and regards them as theatrical. Assure him that the complete absence of gesture is still *more* unnatural, because it suggests that he is made of stone, incapable of moving arms or legs and even of changing facial expression. Train him to let his arms hang naturally, not stiffly, and to move fluently from this position into the most frequently used gesture—pointing to a slide. The ability to locate and point to a portion of a slide while continuing to face the audience and to speak smoothly and coherently is fundamental to good oral presentation.

Ask your students to observe their colleagues in an informal conference. A man smoking a pipe or holding a pencil will gesture with it from time to time to emphasize a point; such gestures are spontaneous and come as a result of his concentration on what he is saying. Some gestures gracefully underline the speaker's words; others, even though unrelated to the subject matter, are somehow reassuring. Gestures in an informal talk should give an equally natural impression, although in point of fact they must be on a larger scale in a lecture theatre if they are not to appear puny or perfunctory.

Nervous Tension

It is natural for any speaker to feel some nervous tension when he faces an audience. A certain amount may actually be beneficial by acting as a mental spur. However, nervous gestures and visibly quaking knees disturb the audience. A rostrum is a handy gadget for concealing nervousness and awkward posture, but it should not be clung to as though in desperation. Absolute mastery of one's feelings seldom comes even with much practice in public speaking. However, there are ways to reduce nervousness. The most important one, of course, is to know the subject thoroughly, to be completely sure of the outline, and to have prepared and rehearsed so thoroughly that absolutely nothing major can go wrong.

Advise a student not to start speaking as soon as he reaches the platform; instead, tell him to relax by taking several deep breaths. Then have him concentrate on his outline, pause slightly between paragraphs, and speak deliberately but in a normal tone of voice. Remind him that the listeners are sympathetic and want him to do his best. At worst, they are neutral toward him personally, having come in the hope of gleaning useful information. A single warm, friendly smile at the beginning does wonders to relax both the speaker and the audience.

Timing

As timing is so important, timing marks should be inserted into the organizational plan of the talk; changed, if necessary, during each rehearsal by a colleague listening with stop-watch in hand; and finally marked in red on the file cards used for the performance. If nervousness has made the speaker go faster or slower during the actual talk than during the rehearsal sessions, the timing marks will bring this to his attention early enough to make the appropriate correction.

A speaker who is neither hurrying nor dallying requires about one minute for 120 words. The equivalent of a double-spaced typewritten page will take roughly 2½ minutes to present. This allows time for brief pauses after important points.

A technique used by news commentators and other professional speakers will stand all speakers in good stead: rather than using a simple period at the end of each sentence, they place a series of periods at the end of principal thoughts. These are reminders to pause and allow time for audience comprehension.

Getting off the Platform

When inexperienced speakers realize they are nearing the end of a talk, they are likely to speed up the rate of delivery as though they cannot wait to finish and rush off—which, indeed, may well be the case!

Because the end of a speech should be its strongest point, the conclusion should be rounded out and the final sentence delivered in a firm voice. Train a student to avoid asking for questions when he finishes. In the first place, this is the chairman's responsibility; second, it precludes applause; and third, it takes the listeners' thoughts away from the speaker's final sentence.

Taking one step back after the final words and looking at the chairman is a good plan. This enables the speaker to pick up his outline during the applause and saves him from the final indignity of having to retrieve cards or papers that can be scattered far and wide by a hasty retreat.

Rehearsal

An instructor can render a lasting service to his students not only by convincing them of the importance of thorough preparation for oral communication, but also by providing opportunities for practice in giving talks. A first step in developing effective speaking techniques is to organize working sessions in which one student gives a 10-minute talk, with the rest of the class *at the back* of a lecture room to serve as audience. Familiarity with the subject is the best way to avoid nervousness, so topics should be carefully selected—one that ties in with part of a student's major assignment from the writing course, or a description of some other research he has conducted, or a "journal club" presentation summarizing one or more papers in which the speaker is particularly interested. You can gain the confidence of your class and create an atmosphere of constructive criticism by leading off with a 10-minute talk yourself and inviting criticism. If you don't want your self-image to be too badly bruised, insert some deliberate errors in both speech and slides to permit the criticism to have a starting point and a focus.

When tape recorders are available, they should be recommended for solo rehearsal sessions. Their usefulness is, however, limited, because the delivery may sound slow to the practicing student when actually it is the proper speed for audience absorption.

Classroom practice sessions serve a function that no amount of solitary practice can. They provide the "live" audience essential for rehearsing eye contact, gestures, and other aspects of platform ease. The question-and-answer period following his presentation can pinpoint the weaknesses in a student's talk, particularly by showing him the points he failed to make clear and those he should have emphasized more.

There will be times when questions directed to the speaker strike him as stupid or even malicious. Tell him to make sure he has heard the question correctly. Asking that it be repeated also gives him additional time to marshal his thoughts and phrase his response. If a courteous and informative reply is not accepted, the speaker can suggest meeting his questioner later so they can go into more detail without bogging down the session or running over the allotted time.

The question period can also prepare him for the shock of an unresponsive audience. It is most disheartening to conclude what one feels was an effective presentation and have total silence in response to the chairman's request for questions. One question is usually all it takes to get an audience started. The student will do well to furnish one or two of his close friends with questions he would like to be asked. Their questions not only get things moving but also give him an opportunity to provide more detail on a point than time limitations allowed in his formal presentation. This device, incidentally, is often employed at large-scale congresses by scientists who have gained recognition as effective speakers.

Criticism of a student's initial efforts should come mainly from the instructor and they should be constructive. Greater frankness can come later! Class seminars make a useful forum in which the fledgling speaker can gain confidence before venturing farther afield, and they prepare him for the unsuspected hazards of oral presentation—the disappearing chalk, the unadjustable microphone, slides that persist in being out of order or upside down, and fainting or other disturbances in the audience.

Something that students find most surprising is that success in presenting serious, scholarly work depends to a considerable extent on techniques borrowed from the theatre. Coach the shyest and most introspective of your students to give his short talk in an overemphatic, theatrical way, with a degree of projection that he considers inappropriate, and ask for the class's reactions. If the lecture room is any bigger than a classroom, the chances are that the class will think it a refreshingly clear performance, not in the least exaggerated. Even the tape recording will reveal to the distrustful performer that he is by no means a candidate for an Oscar, but has merely given—perhaps for the first time in his life—a talk with the firm, strong delivery that it deserves.

APPENDIX TO CHAPTER 13

Examples of possible openings for the topic *The Epidemiology of Frostbite*, suitable for many different types of audience.

The Narrative

"The typical sergeant in Korea during the winter of 1951–52 was a mother hen. He coaxed, pleaded, cajoled, and ordered his men to change their socks often, to cleanse their feet as often as possible, to keep moving their toes and fingers as much as possible when pinned down by enemy fire. A man so eager to have his men do such things is not likely to forget to do them himself. Small wonder, then, that the rate of frostbite among sergeants *as identical risks* was 4.2 per 1,000 compared to 13.0 for privates."

Rhetorical Question

"Why did so many American fighting men suffer frostbite in Korea during the winter of 1950? Was it because Uncle Sam was unprepared? Was it that Uncle Sam just didn't care?"

Startling Statement

"Alcohol is the most successful protection against frostbite—alcohol taken internally and in large quantities. Or so we might be led to believe from newspaper stories of drunks who peacefully survived a night in an alley under winter temperatures that could be expected to kill an average person."

Negative Statement

"Improved standards of clothing developed on the basis of World War II did not prevent cold injury during the Korean conflict. Improved equipment designed for better operation in freezing temperatures did not prevent cold injury during the Korean conflict. And training techniques in effect from the lessons of World War II failed to prevent cold injury during the Korean conflict."

Comparison or Contrast

"The United States Army often awards the Purple Heart to soldiers who have incurred frostbite. The British Army is more apt to slap their men with a charge of malingering."

Reference to Audience's Dominant Interest

"All of you here this morning have a special interest in cold injury. Some of you have made important contributions to that general area, either by categorizing degrees of severity of injury or by delineating treatment regimes. But I wonder how many of you have given thought to such subtle modifying factors as fatigue and morale."

Listing of Specific Instances

"A frontline rifleman is more apt to suffer frostbite than a cook at Division headquarters. An inadequately clad soldier is much more susceptible to frostbite than one who is warmly clad. But how do we explain the fact that one soldier suffers frostbite while another, wearing the same type of combat clothing and in the same immediate locale, does not? What, in insurance language, is it that makes one a better risk than another?"

Gradual Narrowing of Broad Statement

"Weather conditions during the 1950 police action in Korea were probably the most severe ever faced by the American fighting man. Winter temperatures were lower than those in Europe during World War I or in either Europe or the Aleutians during World War II."

Descriptive Opening

"For the first time in field research into cold injury under combat conditions, finite temperatures and wind speeds were measured along the front lines. The separation of data according to intensity of combat permitted formulas to be devised that were reasonably reliable in predicting the incidence of frostbite under other conditions."

Historical Approach

"Historical reference to cold injury in war goes back many centuries. The armies of Alexander the Great experienced it, as did Napoleon's forces in Russia. Indeed, cold continued to be an effective ally of the Russians in World War II, as can be attested by any German soldier who survived a Russian winter."

14

Principles and Practices in Searching the Scientific Literature

EDITOR'S PREFACE:

This chapter has been placed at the end of the book because it does not fit readily into a course on scientific writing given to advanced graduate students. Clearly, if your students are ready to contemplate writing a journal article they must have been engaged in research for a year or two; they should already be fairly skilled in searching the literature and will have been guided in bibliographic techniques by their individual supervisors at the outset of their research.

But because searching the literature is so closely related to contributing to it, we have included this outline for teaching the subject formally, and suggest these alternative times for offering it:

A. At the beginning of the graduate student's career, as a way of familiarizing him quickly with search techniques and convenient sources of information. Each supervisor of research could teach his new students individually, using this outline, or the instructor in scientific writing could teach a class in general principles as a basis for individual supervisors' later refinement.

B. As part of the course on scientific writing in the student's second or third year of research. The material would then come as reinforcement or review of whatever guidance was provided at the beginning of the research. Two fresh approaches can now be employed, both because of the student's experience in library work and because of his exposure to the principles and process of scientific writing. In one, the instructor concentrates on the *writing* that the literature searcher does in the library: effective note-taking, combination of the conclusions of several papers into a short survey, and all other kinds of critical analysis on paper—with reference to the principle that *writing clarifies thinking*. The other approach is to get the students to analyze the difficulties they encounter in their search and thereby define how the author of a journal article, by taking appropriate thought as he writes, can facilitate a searcher's access to the information and ideas he will publish. In designing his title, abstract, and key indexing terms, the student will then have a more extensive audience in mind than those who will read his article immediately on publication, and in one more way he will be trained to do a better job of writing a journal article than before he followed this course.

YOU SHOULD READ:

Mudge, I.G. Introduction (1936) to his *Guide to Reference Books* (6th ed.), now published as 2nd supplement to the 9th edition of the *Guide to Reference Books* (E. P. Sheeny, ed.). 1982. American Library Association, Chicago.

Olle, J. G. *A Guide to Sources of Information in Libraries*. 1984. Gower, Aldershot, England.

NOTE: References on the subject of searching the scientific literature offer either general principles or certain specific pieces of information, such as comments on *Index Bergeyana* for bacterial nomenclature. Few, if any, specific guidelines on "how to do it" are to be found for a search of a single narrow field, such as the literature on food additives. To assist moderately specialized students, you might explore:

Biological

Kerker, A. E., and H. T. Murphy. *Biological and Biomedical Resource Literature*. 1968. Purdue University, Lafayette, Ind.

Wyatt, H. V. *Information Sources in the Life Sciences*. 1986. Butterworths, London.

Medical

Huth, E. J. *How to Write and Publish Papers in the Medical Sciences*. 1982. ISI Press, Philadelphia. pp. 11–36.

Morton, L. T. *How to Use a Medical Library*. 6th ed. 1952. Heinemann Medical, London. (Primarily for British users.)

Morton, L. T. and Godbolt, S. *Information Sources in the Medical Sciences*. 3rd ed. 1983. Butterworths, Sevenoaks, Kent.

Chemical

Bottle, R. T. (ed.) *Use of the Chemical Literature*. 3rd ed. 1979. Butterworths, Sevenoaks, Kent; Shoe String Press, Hamden, CO.

Burman, C. R. *How to Find Out in Chemistry.* 2nd ed. 1967. Pergamon Press, Oxford and New York.

Mathematical

Pemberton, J. E. *How to Find Out in Mathematics.* 2nd ed. 1979. Pergamon Press, Oxford and New York.

Although searching the literature is long established as the scientist's way of ensuring that he knows what others have done in the experimental quest for knowledge, the budding behavioral sciences have not as yet produced a theory of search. Habits and patterns of searching the literature vary with individual inquiries, interests, settings, resources, temperaments, schedules, and budgets in the world of science.

There seems to be, then, no single "right way" to search the literature and keep up to date with it. Nevertheless, there are some valid general principles of search, and by enunciating them you can help each student to choose his own tactics wisely, in the full knowledge of what is available and what is likely to suit him best. Emphasize that he has a multitude of alternatives and should choose among them deliberately. I have arranged this chapter in two sections—*Principles* and *Practices*—in the hope that you, too, will pick and choose, selecting from both sections what seems most appropriate and useful for your class. Similarly, the assignments are suggested at logical places in the text but need not be assigned in this order or, indeed, used at all unless you have the time and the wish to illustrate the particular points to which they refer.

Variations in search patterns depend not only on the factors mentioned above but also on the phase of search. At the earliest phase, search is exploratory. It may begin with the reading of a review to develop direction and perspective. The oriented reader will then zero in on a favored target with the aid of a bibliography chosen as a result of this preliminary reading. When he has selected the area in which research seems called for and likely to be fruitful, he will develop a hypothesis and then look specifically for accounts of previous work that bears on this hypothesis. Finally, he must keep up with new findings. In this phase, he consults colleagues, reads specialized journals, and screens abstracts. The selection of a special subject may sharply reduce the volume of literature he feels he should cover. Even for browsing outside the chosen field, a few outstanding journals usually enable the reader to follow the mainstream of science. Screening techniques and other search devices can help the student mine and refine the literary ore.

While the teacher is wise to emphasize that search of the literature must precede experiment, it may also be useful to caution the student against being discouraged when he finds that his best ideas seem to have been preempted by his elders. If his question is well conceived, it is probable that he will find some aspect of it that may be untouched or that requires re-examination, for the published literature is not without flaws. In that case the search, far from being fruitless, will have provided the necessary background for continuing investigation. In any event, the student should be encouraged to pursue a line of inquiry that promises to open new avenues as he progresses.

If you are giving a self-contained course on searching the literature, you may like to entitle it "Use of the Literature Before, During, and At the End of a Piece of Research," in order to emphasize how search technique changes with the phase of research. If, on the other hand, you are adding the "search" sessions to the writing course described in Part 1 of this manual, the point at which you choose to insert this instruction (see the preface to this chapter) will affect which type of search strategy you will concentrate on. I mention these considerations here because your approach to the subject should be clearly defined before you begin to teach it.

Principles

1. Allow Enough Time.

A major pitfall in searching is a failure to allow enough time to obtain the papers selected. From the time the title and source are submitted to the librarian it may take from two weeks to six months to obtain the text. Even more time must be allowed if translation is required. The practical value of Assignment 5, below, is that it may impress a student with the need for timing his requests for literature.

2. Verify. Verify. Verify.

As a cardinal principle of search, emphasize how important it is to verify sources. You may wish to quote Place (1) on verification, in association with Assignment 6, (p. 177):

"A common fault lies in taking a reference from another's bibliography as though it were thereby Gospel truth. . . . Take no reference for granted. Verify the reference that your best friend gives you. Verify the reference that your revered chief gives you. Verify, most of all, the reference that you yourself found and jotted down. To err is human, to verify is necessary."

3. Sharpen the Question.

Help students learn to be clear and precise about the subject of search, its limitations, the period to be covered, the sources of probable interest, and the eventual use of the information. Teach them to specify such details as:

languages they will read;
organism by sex and age;
medications (if applicable) with dose limits in quantity, frequency, and duration;
geographical boundaries of the research or applications;
population;
publication years;

and, perhaps, specific sources.

Discuss well-defined projects, such as methods for a patent search, obtaining a reference for a particular statement, organizing an annotated bibliography, preparing a critical review, or seeking an indicator organism as a basis for experiment.

Demonstrate, with a few case histories, that sources of literature (libraries and source books) are not necessarily organized to produce specific answers to specific questions.

Discuss the effect of the *phrasing of the question* ("Is water desalination practical?" versus "What was published in 1966 on desalination costs?") and the *nature of the resource* (the Library of Congress versus the *New York Times Inaex*) on the quantity and relevance of information that may be retrieved. Contrast a search for a cure for scurvy or for the melting-point of a synthetic derivative with a search for treatment of hypertension.

Assignment 1

Let each student frame a question for library search and prepare either an annotated bibliography or a set of quotations, with reference to the sources. It will be desirable to limit the bibliography or note collection to one that can be compiled in one to two hours, based on literature indexed in one year.

Discuss the effectiveness of the questions, preferably with the assistance of an experienced librarian. Explain the process of negotiating the question with the librarian as an important phase of search, so that students will realize that the librarian is trying to be helpful when the question is reviewed. Urge students to pose questions that represent their real interests, not mere exercises (see Assignment 4).

Authorities agree that note-taking and the recording of sources is essential to literature search, but they do not agree on the best method of keeping these records. Some prefer cards, 3 x 5 or 5 x 8 inches; some prefer notebooks, loose-leaf or otherwise; some like loose paper slips; some use pens of various colors; some photocopy the text.

ASSIGNMENT 2

Propose that, after a week or so of browsing, students bring in their notes and compare methods of note-taking, including the form of citation (see Assignment 4).

4. KNOW YOUR SOURCES.

It may be helpful to consider the literature in three categories: encyclopedic, including directories, bibliographies, handbooks, reference tables, and various kinds of dictionaries; books or monographs, including manuals, guides, textbooks, reviews, and reports of special commissions; and collections of articles, including primary journals and proceedings of conferences and symposia.

A well-selected list of encyclopedic sources, books, and basic journals, can have practical value to the graduate student, but stress selection for relevance, currency, and accessibility. (A selected bibliography of medical reference works, 1679–1966, distributed by the Medical Library Association, contains more than 2700 titles.)

Many university scientists collaborate with a librarian to identify and obtain the search aids most useful to their departments. The librarian, in turn, can introduce graduate students to the sources currently available and to their limitations and uses.

(If a librarian is available, this is a good spot for a guest lecturer on the resources of the local library for scientific investigations. Ideally, the talk should be in the library itself, where each reference source may be examined and the other facilities may be used.)

Trelease puts the use of the library at the forefront of the process of scientific research (pp. 3–11) and follows with a course of action for exploring the literature (pp. 11–25). In logical order, he prescribes (a) textbooks and monographs, (b) reviews (the National Library of Medicine publishes an index of medical reviews), (c) yearbooks or similar works, (d) abstract and index journals, (e) current literature, (f) original articles, and (g) guides to the literature, which he lists for respective scientific disciplines in the succeeding ten pages.

To this course of action, one may add the possibility of obtaining special bibliographies for the topic under review, sometimes by automated printout. The "demand bibliographies" obtainable from MEDLARS provide an example (Medical Literature Analysis and Retrieval Service, details given in *Guide To MEDLARS Services,* National Library of Medicine, Bethesda, MD).

A classic on the approach to using reference materials is Mudge's introduction to the ALA's *Guide to Reference Books*, 6th ed. (see p. 168). Mudge proposes a series of steps for the reader who desires to learn the intelligent use of reference books. These steps include:

1. Examine title page carefully for information as to:
   a) scope of work as indicated in title
   b) author's name
   c) author's previous record
   d) publisher
   e) date (while dates of copyright or preface do not guarantee the date of the information in the book, they help to place it, especially if they are earlier than the date of publication)
2. Read preface or introduction for:
   a) further information as to scope
   b) special features claimed
   c) limitations, if any
   d) comparison with other books on the same subject
3. Examine book itself for:
   a) arrangement
   b) kind of entry
   c) cross references, i.e., the extent to which these are included, and whether they are given in the main work or in a separate list

d) supplementary lists, noting their number and kind and how they are connected with the main work
e) indexes, noting fullness and exactness of reference
f) quality and kind of articles (scientific, signed, impartial, documented. Trustworthiness and accuracy are fundamental to the value of the work.)

The full text of Mudge's advice warrants careful study.

5. Eye the Index.

Even in allied disciplines, index headings differ. For example, ecology means one thing to a sociologist, something else to a biologist. An item listed under Toxins in one index may turn up in another only under Poisons. An earnest searcher does not give up after reviewing one heading but looks into other possible associations. Explain how the selection (quality) and number (depth) of index terms affect search and retrieval.

(If available, a professional indexer or other expert in library automation might be invited to tell what the user needs to know about using automated storage, searching, and retrieval techniques. The exercise on framing a question, above, was aimed at the usual manual search. A question intended for an automated search will need some special treatment.)

6. Discriminate.

A search should not dig into every title listed, but should concentrate on the items that promise to yield relevant data. Warn students that titles may be misleading and that the reputation of the author is often a better guide. At the same time, stress the importance, when the searcher turns into an author, of composing descriptive titles, especially to support automatic indexing and searching.

The exercise of discrimination is tied to the prescription to Sharpen the Question. Students may enjoy the experience of applying discrimination to the selection of references according to titles. Let us take an example. Given a choice of titles on Statistics, the reader seeking an introduction to the subject can only guess which of the following would be best to consult:

Introduction to Probability and Statistics
Handbook of Probability and Statistics with Tables
Introduction to Statistical Analysis

Statistical Analysis of Experimental Data
Introduction to Theory of Statistics

He may have more to go on if his interest in statistics is related to an animal experiment, as the following titles suggest:

The Design of Experiments
Statistical Methods for Research Workers
Statistical Methods Applied to Experiments in Agriculture and Biology

The following titles suggest special qualifications in themselves:

Mathematics Essential to Elementary Statistics
Say It With Figures
Graphic Charts Handbook
Handbook of Graphic Presentation
Statistical Sources
Statistical Tables for Biological, Agricultural, and Medical Research

In the first batch of titles given above, the reader's discrimination will be based less on the title than on appraisal of the author's position, publications, and reputation. The reader will also consider the book's recency and durability. An updated classic that has gone through many editions, for example, may be a better bet than a relatively untested modern work.

In the second batch, the third title is the most specific and will therefore be the one most quickly selected or discarded.

In the third batch, all depends on whether the reader is asking "What do I need to know to study statistics?" (title 1); "What are good methods of presenting statistics?" (titles 2–4); or "Where can I find a handy set of reference tables?" (titles 5, 6). Item 4 is the title that points most directly to methods of presentation, unless the reader happens to know that "Say It With Figures" is especially well regarded.

ASSIGNMENT 3

Using bibliographies obtained in Assignment 1, let students identify the titles that appear most nearly suited to their interests. Have each student then report whether investigation confirms his expectations, title by title. Each may submit the results in tabular form, but the experience may also lead to some profitable discussion of both the selection and construction of titles.

7. Give Up In Time.

Pique or stubbornness may seduce a student into wasting hours in a search for a relatively inconsequential piece of information. Or he may pursue a study long after he has passed the point of diminishing returns. For some, a search may prove so attractive an occupation that the investigator is reluctant to leave it for the duties of the bench and desk. Searchers should recognize this deflection of aim as a potential danger and discipline themselves to ask at frequent intervals "Should I stop now?" Like the gold prospector, the searcher may be obsessed by the feeling that the big strike is under the next rock. But reason, and a calm assessment of the cost/benefit ratio of his endeavors, may rescue him from the psychological forces of compulsion and obsession.

8. Create a Useful Product.

Ideally, the bibliography gained by the search should consist of citations written neatly on cards suitable for filing. Entries should be legible enough for a typist to copy accurately. The form should be consistent, and the annotations explicit. (The current condition of titles suggests that a bibliography without annotations is less functional than a bikini without a girl.) The needs of the reader must be considered as well as those of the investigator, and when the bibliography is reproduced as part of a publication the citations must be both complete and accurate.

Assignment 4

Let students exchange the notes they made in Assignment 2 and then rate each other for legibility, consistency of form in citation, and quality of the annotations. This exercise should demonstrate the value of creating a useful product. Preparation of a useful bibliography could be assigned in association with other exercises.

Practices

So much for principles. What are actual practices? Some people dote on abstracts. Others are satisfied with nothing but the full text of the original papers, which they locate from an index, an announcement, references in other papers, or the latest *Current Contents.* Many a search is started with a personal conversation, and it broadens and deepens as its importance engages the questioner in hot pursuit. Through his library, a reader may ask for a bibliographical search at the National Library of Medicine. Or he may be content with the local library catalog, the indexes, the abstracting journals, and whatever else is at hand. He may try to evaluate a document by looking into *Science Citation Index* to see how much it is used as a reference. This source will also lead to the most recent publications that cite the document and which may therefore be reporting new work in the same field. If he is stumped for an answer from the literature, he may consult the National Referral Center for Science and Technology at the Library of Congress or its directories, or he may find a helpful source in Dornay, B.A. (ed.) *Directory of Special Libraries and Information Centers in the USA and Canada,* 8th ed. 1983 (Gale Research, Detroit).

Assignment 5

It may be instructive for the student to keep a record of his specific library requests, the time required for a response, or the reasons for any lack of response. (Failures and delays in library responses have encouraged many institutions to purchase works on demand, rather than borrow from a central library, especially if the works are new. The saving in time and effort compensates for the cost of the purchase.) Analysis of the failures can guide the searcher in improving request procedures: he may discover that he has inadvertently given the wrong spelling of the author's name, such as Lawton for Lewton; that he has cited the wrong journal—*Chemical Education* instead of *Chemical Documentation;* that he has erred on the date or volume number; that his script is easily misread; or that certain sources are in such heavy demand that it is futile to try to borrow them. Such practical experience is essential for evaluation of the precepts cited above. It also encourages a realistic approach to the art of searching.

Assignment 6

The fallibility of man is such that, with the best of intentions, even a good scientist may misquote or misrepresent. Authors as well as readers should feel an obligation to check the sources. It will be a good learning experience for students who have written papers to review the papers and books given in their references and check them critically against their text. Alternatively, each student can be assigned to check the references in a scientific paper he has read: he may be asked to report on the accuracy of the citations, the accuracy of the quotations or interpretations, the availability of the literature cited, and the average time required to check a reference.

Summary

Search strategy copes chronically with tactical, practical obstacles. In theory, search may saturate the whole human experience. Narrowed down to an investigation of the open literature, search tends to funnel through a single essential portal: the facilities of a scientific library. Skill in using these facilities is acquired by study of the resources and practice in handling them.

In general, students may benefit from help in sharpening their questions, learning reference aids and other sources, studying indexing forms, discriminating among sources, rationing time, and aiming at a useful product. In the main, however, teachers should remember that the student will learn to swim only when he is wet. Once he is persuaded to leap into the library, he will make many random, wasteful efforts. He may even be in danger of drowning in the literary flood unless he is carefully coached in the art of identifying, selecting, screening, and searching the literature. The proper coaching can save his scientific life.

Reference

1. Place, F., Jr. Verify your references. *N.Y. Med. J.*, 1916; 104:697-699. (Note: the name of this journal was later changed to *New York State Journal of Medicine*.)

BIBLIOGRAPHY OF FURTHER READING

You should, in the first place, become thoroughly acquainted with all the books given on p. 56 as the students' reading list. Because you are interested in writing you will enjoy the outstanding books by Quiller-Couch, Gowers, and Lucas, and will wonder why they have not been required reading for the students. The reason is that they deal in depth with literary style, which as we have seen is not an essential part of scientific writing. One aim of the teacher of scientific writing should be, we believe, to deemphasize the stylistic element, which has been overstressed in the student's past and is too easily dismissed by him as of minor importance—unfortunately, too often, along with all other considerations in writing. Tichy's book is less likely to antagonize the determined anti-literary student, and her Chapters 2, 3, 5, and 6 will neatly underline and amplify what you have had to say about organizing.

At the head of most chapters is a reading list of special interest to you in teaching that chapter. These references are not repeated here. What follows is a short list of titles you may like to dip into for further reading and use as sources of examples.

Barrass, R. *Scientists Must Write: A Guide to Better Writing for Scientists, Engineers and Students*. 1978. Chapman & Hall, London; Wiley, New York

Barrass, R. *Students Must Write: A Guide to Better Writing in Course Work and Examinations*. 1982. Methuen, New York and London

These two books by Barrass are well differentiated by their titles; the second may be useful in connection with the writing of theses and dissertations (see Chapter 11) and for students who have particular difficulty in expressing themselves even after you have taught them a scientific method for revising and polishing their style (Chapter 6).

Graves, H.F. and Hoffman, L.S.S. *Report Writing*, 4th ed. 1965. Prentice-Hall, Englewood Cliffs, NJ, and London

Concerned largely with technical and business reports, which have somewhat different requirements from scientific articles, this book nevertheless has a good style chapter that is applicable to scientific writing. The chapter closes with exercises—sentences and paragraphs to be revised—which might form useful assignments.

Harrison, J. (ed.). *Scientists as Writers*. 1965. The M.I.T. Press, Cambridge, MA.; Methuen, London.

Like most anthologies in the field, this one is composed of pieces of *science* writing, i.e., writings by scientists for nonscientist readers. It may broaden your students' perspective and it will show them what good straightforward expository style is, but it will not teach them to write a journal article. The excerpts are thoughtfully commented on by the authors.

Hodges, J. C. and Whitten, M. E. *Harbrace College Handbook,* 9th ed. 1982. Harcourt Brace Jovanovich, New York.

A classic in the field of English language usage. Clearly organized, concise, and easy to use. Contains answers to most questions of grammar, mechanics of writing, and punctuation.

Jones, W. P. and Keene, M. L. *Writing Scientific Papers and Reports*. 8th ed. 1981. Wm. C. Brown, Dubuque, IA.

This book is intended as a text for an undergraduate course in scientific writing, and as such does not attempt to introduce the student to full-scale scholarly publication. "The intention is rather to confront students with a number of simple problems in scientific exposition and to give them instruction and practice in organizing ideas and communicating them to the reader." Teachable discussions of scientific method and logical thinking come, appropriately, at the beginning of the book and an excellent chapter (Chapter 19) on sentence structure and diction, appropriately, at the end.

Chapter 19 will provide you with a wealth of material either for individual guidance or for classes on Grammatical Refinements. If you are cajoled into giving these take, for example, Jones's basic classification on parallelism and balanced sentences, teach your students to use them correctly, and then widen their horizons by showing them examples (from Lucas, Graves and Hodge, or the anthologies by Harrison or Jones and Durham) in which the writer has used parallel constructions not only correctly but triumphantly.

Judd, K. *Copyediting: A Practical Guide*. 1982. Kaufmann, Los Angeles, CA.

Although neither you nor your students need to know much about copyediting, the insights into the technicalities of publishing (as distinct from the conceptual interaction between journal editor and author) provided by this excellent little book may strengthen your background knowledge to enable you to answer questions which may arise when you are teaching Chapter 9.

Kapp, Reginald O. *The Presentation of Technical Information*. 1948. The Macmillan Co., New York; Constable, London.

The preface is excellent, in that it describes the deterrent suggestions encountered by one who proposes to teach scientific writing.

"I was told, for instance, that the whole of the ground ought to be covered at school. I was also advised to abandon the idea of a special course in presentation and, instead, to use the laboratory reports as basis for training the students in the art of exposition, going over each student's report with him sentence by sentence.

"These suggestions revealed a serious under-estimation of the magnitude of the problems that the executive engineer or scientist has to solve in the course of his professional work when he is presenting technical information or reasoned argument. These problems simply do not arise in such elementary factual statements as are contained in a student's laboratory reports. They are not problems in grammar and syntax. They are rarely problems in literary style. They are most often problems in logic and psychology. Teach a man to think clearly, and he is likely to express himself clearly; teach him to think about the person addressed, and he will have learnt the first lesson in the art of conveying information effectively from mind to mind. But teach him only to turn out well-constructed sentences and he may fail badly in the art of exposition."

In the four lectures that follow, the author teaches elementary logical and psychological principles in terms of a metaphorical storekeeper keeping watch over the brain or memory in which information is stored. This method of teaching fails to have lasting impact, however, because it is not related closely enough to the students' everyday activity; it is not linked to enough specific examples; and it does not demand the students' participation. It can succeed only if the teacher commands a language like Quiller-Couch's, so that the lectures are enjoyed at the time, and read frequently afterwards, for their literary excellence and their gusto. Dr. Kapp does not have this command, and so the text is a little flat. Although the author is distinctly on the side of the angels, therefore, his harp playing is not going to ravish and reform the renegade scientific writer.

Kirkman, J. *Good Style for Scientific and Engineering Writing*. 1980. Pitman, London.

Rathbone, Robert R. *Communicating Technical Information*. 1966. Addison-Wesley Publishing Co., Reading, MA, and London.

Short and lively, the book iterates main principles in the name of communicating ideas instead of merely writing them down. The author may provide you with many vivid devices for making your students remember the principles you are trying to convey. Excellent further reading is suggested at the ends of chapters and in the annotated bibliography.

The author has forced the titles of all the chapters into a single form beginning with the definite article: let the resultant artificiality be a warning to you not to resort to such "cute tricks" in teaching. Graduate students in science believe that life is real and earnest, and they do not appreciate the kind of approach in which "The Inadequate Abstract" and "The Improper Introduction" are succeeded, apparently purely for esthetic reasons, by "The Ubiquitous Noise" and "The Neglected Pace."

Reynolds, L. and Simmonds, D. *Presentation of Data in Science*. 1981. Martinus Nijhoff, The Hague

Additional material for Chapter 10.

Richards, I.T. and Richards, P.I. *Proper Words in Proper Places*, rev. ed. 1965. The Christopher Publishing House, Boston.

A well-written reiteration of the necessity for thinking and planning before writing. "*Part 1*: Strategy" in particular may provide reinforcement, if this should be needed, of the principles behind the early steps in writing a journal article.

Turk, C. and Kirkman, J. *Effective Writing: Improving Scientific, Technical and Business Communication*. 1982. Spon, London.

Weisman, H.M. *Basic Technical Writing*, 4th ed. 1980. Charles E. Merrill Books, Columbus, OH; Prentice-Hall, London.

A thorough treatment suitable for a specialist planning a career as a technical writer. The chapters on Scientific Method and Approach; Technical Style, Mechanics, and Grammar; Graphic Presentation; and The Technical Article and Paper will be of special value to you. A wealth of examples of complete papers and their revision is provided. The tone throughout is direct and unpretentious, but the author cannot conceal his depth of scholarship.

Williams, J.M. *Style: Ten Lessons in Clarity and Grace*. 1981. Scott, Foresman & Co., Glenview, IL.

This book, written primarily for the mature writer, explains how to overcome the problem of an unnecessarily complex prose style. Exercises for the reader are scattered throughout the book and suggested answers are given at the back.

Woodford, F.P. Sounder thinking through clearer writing. *Science*. 1967; 156:743-745.

A diatribe against the low standard of writing currently found acceptable in scientific journals, and a plea for graduate courses in scientific writing such as the one you are planning to give.

SUBJECT INDEX